Introducing:

The Super Clever Advanced Learning Method (SCALM)

A Universal Method to Learn Any Subject and to Memorize Entire Books!

By

Chris M Nemo

This book is dedicated to…

My late Father and Mother

(G. and I.I.)

I love you with all my heart
and miss you every day!

Table of Contents

Introduction

Thank you for your purchase of my introductory book on the Super Clever Advanced Learning Method (SCALM). You're one step closer to becoming a Super Learner, because the most important promise of this book is that you can become one!

All it takes is a little motivation and a method to facilitate your learning. This book will teach you the method step by step, and I am sure that, after you will see how easy the learning process becomes for you, your motivation will come by itself.

In this book, I want to present to you **my original and extremely efficient method** for learning any kind of information, a very versatile method that combines the most efficient memory techniques.

I created this method after many years in which I had to learn a lot of abstract and highly diversified information. At one point, I asked myself the question: "*How could I approach in a unitary way the memorization of any kind of information, whether it is a biology essay or a philosophy book? What are the universal steps of any learning process and how can I adapt them to any type of material that I have to learn?"*

The answer came when I began to study and practice memory techniques. I discovered that, by combining these techniques, not only did the learning process become faster but at the same time the learned information remained much longer stored in my memory.

Over time, I became a proactive learner and I synthesized a series of steps that transformed my learning into a pleasant and extremely effective experience.

There is a method—a formula if you will—behind any Ultra-Efficient Learning. And that's what this book is all about: taking you behind the curtain and showing you that formula.

Indeed, this great learning tool, that I have named *"the Super Clever Advanced Learning Method (SCALM)"* is extremely effective because of its versatility. It can be applied to any type of material you will have to remember.

If you search on Google: *"which are the most effective learning techniques"*, you will find a ranking of the 10 most known techniques, ordered by their efficiency, and you will find that the most effective care based on practicing the learned concepts. But what do we do if we have to learn abstract things, without practical applicability, as is the case with over 90% of the information we need to learn throughout our studies or in our professional life?

The SCALM technique comes with a new approach, meant to transform abstract notions into concrete things and unintelligible concepts into easily memorable images, by combining the most efficient memory techniques invented by mental athletes for memory competitions. These extremely advanced, but at the same time easy to learn and to apply techniques, make also the SCALM method very easy to understand and to use, once you understand the principles on which it is based.

This method solves the problem of memorizing abstract information through a series of simple steps that will turn hundreds of pages of intricate information into easy-to-remember images.

What is truly spectacular about the SCALM method is that it can help you memorize entire books. This doesn't mean that it offers you a miraculous solution to memorize information, as many photo-reading techniques claim to do. The SCALM learning process involves a work of deconstructing, organizing, and reconstructing (recoding) the material, all these stages being part of the natural process of efficient learning.

In simple terms, it translates the abstract information into the alphabet of the brain, which is made up of concrete images, thus making it possible to memorize it in the long term.

I must say that the SCALM learning is by no means Rote Memorization, because it transforms a lot of random data into a memorable construct, like a digital album of memorable images for the brain and because it works directly with the brain's grammar, which is made up of images.

By following a series of clear steps and simple rules for memorizing different types of information, The SCALM technique brings a systematic approach to a task that seems difficult for all of us: *memorizing hundreds of pages of horribly abstract, unattractive and unrelated information.*

I have to tell you from the beginning that this is not a theoretical book. Although I will try to explain in detail each concept and each step of this simple method, I hope this book will not seem very theoretical to you. I will try to add as many examples as possible, to help you better understand how the method works.

You might view this book as an opportunity to improve your proactive learning abilities and to add to your learning toolset an invaluable technique.

In the following pages, I will show you how this method works and we will start with an introductory example and I'm sure you'll be amazed at the ease with which you can learn new things using the SCALM method. That being said, *let's dive indirectly to the SCALM learning process.*

PART I: The SCALM Learning Process

Chapter One: Meet the SCALM Technique

The essence of the SCALM techniques consists of the deconstruction, organization, and then reconstruction of the material, so that it is brought into a memorable form for you. For this purpose, it contains 5 steps, and "SCALM" is an acronym for these steps, which are:

- Structure
- Chunk
- Associate
- Locate
- Memorize.

The first step of the method is to **Structure the information**. This stage aims to create an overview of the material to be memorized, which will help us to organize the memorization process. In short, at this stage we create a general map of what we have to do.

There are cases where the material is already organized by the author in the form of tables, charts, or lists, and we can use these as an overview of the information. Of course, all books also have a table of contents, but it is often difficult to use because of its text form. For this reason, the SCALM technique often uses a very efficient tool, invented by the great memory and learning expert Tony Buzan, who is called "*Mind Map*". A Mind Map is a synthetic diagram that provides an overview of the material and helps us organize our memorization process. Basically, in this step, we create a structure that will help us understand how the material is structured, like a tree in which we will hang later the memorable images associated with the learned things.

The second step of the SCALM method is **Chunking**, a process by which the material is broken down into organized and meaningful pieces of information.

You have probably heard the saying that you eat an elephant one bite at a time and this is the principle on which any complex human activity is based. The same principle applies to learning. At this stage, we break down the material into smaller pieces, which will be easier to associate and manipulate in our minds. In the end, we will have a lot of pieces that we then stick like leaves in the tree that is our mind map.

The next step is the **Association.** This is the core of the mental process of memorization. Association is the central element of any memory technique and it means creating a mental connection between the abstract information you have to remember and a concrete image as a person, an object, or an animal. This easy-to-memorize image will act as a trigger to bring the other to light, from the depths of your memory. It works like a shortcut that launches an application from your computer. The "leaves" in our tree take concrete shape and, at the end of this stage, we will have a tree full of simple and concrete pictures (like a horse, a lion, or a king), which we will have to memorize in the next stage.

The fourth stage is **Localization**, which is one of the most important aspects of orderly memorization. You've probably heard so far of *the Memory Palace Method* (also known as "the Loci Method"), an ancient memory technique which is based on placing mental images along an imaginary journey that will become an orderly structure for your memories. If you do not know how it works, you will learn in this book.

In this stage, each branch of our tree, together with its images, will turn into an imaginary journey.

Imagine you go to work and along your route you meet, in some well-defined places, the images you have to remember (for example, you might meet a lion in front of your house or an elephant in the bus station where you wait in the morning). The more theatrical, even strange, or funny the image, the better you can remember it.

This odd combination between a concrete and ordered structure such as your journey to work in the morning and the equally concrete images that you created in the association stage will cause them to become deeply embedded in your memory.

The last step of the SCALM technique is the **Memorization of the Images**. If you applied the method's previous steps correctly and if you created powerful images and triggers for your memories, this step is very simple. You simply walk again in your mind along your route, and all the words will appear in your mind's eye in the same sequence.

Because of the way the SCALM Method is organized, practicing it should help you internalize many memory improvement principles and help you overcome obstacles that prevent you from becoming a Super Learner. You will understand how memory training works and how memory athletes memorize thousands of items when participating in memory competitions. It is the same process of coding into simple and concrete images of abstract concepts (such as numbers, binary numbers, or playing cards), and then placing them along with memory palaces. This book will show you the secrets of memory improvement, as it combines the most effective memory techniques used by mental athletes.

Chapter Two: Meet Johnny

Meet Johnny!

Because of his extraordinary memory, his friends call him "*Johnny Mnemonic*". But Johnny has no cybernetic implant in his brain- to help him memorize so many things.

While his colleagues are indulging in "*smart drugs*", Johnny learns in a natural, systematic and proactive way.

He's just a smart guy who has learned a very effective learning technique and knows how to use his brain to make his life easier. Wherever he goes, he has complete self-confidence in his learning skills, because he carries in his mind an extremely useful tool to help him learn any type of information.

This learning tool, called the Super-Clever-Advanced-Learning-Method or SCALM, helps him to memorize any kind of material: lessons, essays, speeches, and even entire books. In short, he has a universal method that helps him memorize efficiently hundreds of pages of horribly abstract, unattractive, and unrelated information.

Today, Johnny has to learn a geography lesson.

Let's see how he uses the SCALM method to learn this lesson:

First of all, he reads the material and sketches a mind map of it. This way, he has a visual plan of the whole material.

Then, he starts chunking the material into small, easy-to-handle pieces. Thus, the entire material will become easy to use the list of items.

The most important stage of the method is that of association. Each chunk will be transformed into a memorable image like an object, a person, or an animal, by applying a few simple memory techniques.

Here is a chunk that contains a list of items: the 5 Great Lakes (Huron, Ontario Erie, Michigan, and Superior). Johnny will turn it into an easy-to-remember acronym (**"HOMES"**), which he will note next to that chunk.

And here is a larger list that he has to learn: the Central American countries, from North to South(Mexico, Belize, Guatemala, El Salvador, Honduras, Nicaragua, Costa Rica, Panama).

Johnny applies another technique, called *"The Sentence Method"*, and turns this list into an easy-to-remember mnemonic phrase: "***More Big Gorillas Eat Hotdogs, Not Corn Pops"*** and notes it next to that chunk.

Johnny likes hip hop music, and sometimes it comes easy to him to make rhymes or poems, or even short stories, to help him memorize his lists.

Here is how he remembers the year of Christopher Columbus's discovery of the Americas:

"Columbus sailed the ocean blue,

In fourteen hundred and ninety-two."

To remember the 7 Continents, Johnny uses a simple technique called *"The Story method"*.

Here is the little story that will help him remember the continents:

"North America married South America and they went to Europe for their honeymoon. Soon after they had quadruplets who all had A names: Africa, Australia, Asia (who was the biggest, even though he had the shortest name) and Antarctica, the oldest child."

Further, he has to learn a more difficult geographical term, called ***"geosyncline".***

The perfect method for memorizing it is called *"The Sound-Alike technique"* and works by replacing unfamiliar words with other words that sound similar.

For Johnny, "Geosyncline" sounds like *"Joe"* and *"cycling"* and he will remember this term by using the image of ***"Joe Pesci cycling"***

Numbers and data are also easy to memorize for Johnny because he uses a technique that helps him transform them into words and then into memorable images, known as "*The Major system.*"

The length of the Mississippi River (3768 km) will be memorized using the Major system as follows: 3768 is divided into 2 digits (37 and 68), each of them becoming a group of consonants (MK and CF), and then 2 words (Mickey and Coffee). To memorize this number, Johnny will imagine Mikey Mouse with a coffee in his hand, counting "*One Mississippi, Two Mississippi,...*"

The height of Denali, the tallest mountain in North America (6,190 meters) will become the consonants JD and PZ, which can be memorized by imagining *"Judy Garland eating Pizza on the top of this mountain."*

After he transformed the material into images, all he has to do now is to give life to these images, by placing them in familiar places from his life.

For this purpose, Johnny applies a very efficient ancient technique called *"The Memory Palace Method"*, which gives him an orderly structure where to place his mnemonic images.

In his imagination, he places his images along his daily road to school:

"In front of his door he sees two little ***homes*** *reminding him of the great lakes, then, in the middle of the street, he sees* ***two giant gorillas eating hotdogs****, reminding him of the Central American countries.*

Gorillas are hit by a ***ship sailing down the street****, reminding him of Columbus.*

A little further on, in front of the barbershop on the corner of the streets, he sees a family with four children, who reminds him of ***the continents' story****, and then, in the bus station, he imagines* ***Joe Pescy cycling.***

Under the tree in front of the school he sees ***Mikey Mouse with a Starbucks coffee in his hand, counting "One Mississippi, Two Mississippi ..."****, and on the school stairs he imagines* ***Judy Garland eating a slice of pizza.****"*

As you can see, Johnny just turned the abstract information into a cartoon movie.

I think you can imagine how easy it is now for Johnny to memorize these images. He just mentally travels along his way to school, and the pictures will automatically appear there.

For tomorrow's lesson, Johnny will choose another journey, the route he goes through the park when he walks his dog. Any real or mental journey can give Johnny a new memory palace to memorize his lessons.

In a few days, he will give a speech at an event organized by a student association, and of course, he will memorize the speech by applying the SCALM method. The rooms of his house will become a familiar mental palace for the images of his speech.

Here's how easy it is to learn anything using the SCALM method! By following its steps, you can effectively memorize entire books. I'm not saying it's easy, because it involves a work of deconstructing, organizing and reconstructing (re-coding) the material, but in essence, it is very simple and, most of the time, fun to use. We all love cartoons and the SCALM method helps us become the directors of our cartoon mental movies, which helps us learn and memorize in the long run.

We are dealing with a very advanced and effective proactive learning method, but at the same time easy to learn and fun to use. Also, I must tell you that the memory techniques used by the SCALM method are also used by the mental athletes in memory competitions because they are very efficient.

I hope I have convinced you of its value, so I am waiting for you in the next chapters, to learn more about it.

PART II: How (and What) We Learn

Chapter Three: The Memorization Laws

This part is a little more theoretical than the rest of the book, but it has its importance in understanding the SCALM method because it presents the basic concepts of the learning process.

This chapter will briefly present to you how our memory works, in the next chapter I will show you the types of materials we have to learn in our studies, and then, in the 5th chapter, I will present you an overview of the memory techniques used by the SCALM method.

Now, let's see how the learning process happens in our brain:

Learning is a sequential operation where information processing moves from the present (meaning the sensory memory) into short-term memory and eventually moves into long-term memory.

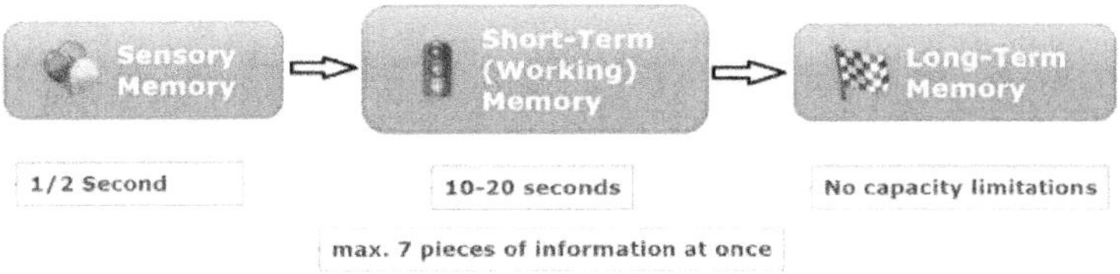

After the perception of an object, the stimuli received through the five senses, activate the **Sensory memory**, an ultra-short-term memory that decays very quickly and who works as a kind of buffer for the raw information, which is retained accurately, but very briefly. As our senses work continuously, sensory memory is constantly fed with new information.Because it has a limited storage capacity, outdated information is quickly replaced with new ones.

Then, the information passes into **Short-term memory**, where it is held for 10-20 seconds. It works like a traffic light intersection. When you are reading a sentence, your short-term memory stores the beginning of the sentence while you are reading the rest of it, so that you can comprehend the whole. It holds the information you are currently thinking about, for between 10 and 20 seconds and usually retains no more than about seven pieces of information at once.

Here, in the Short-term memory, is the starting point for every effective learning technique. By *Observation, Attention,* and *Repetition*, the information can become an unforgettable, long-term memory.

Information that has been well consolidated is finally stored in the **Long-term memory**. Anything that took place more than a couple of minutes ago and you can remember is stored in the long-term memory. In contrast with the two previous memory types, the long term memory has no capacity limitations. Memories such as the stories you read in childhood, the date that you got married, or what you ate today at your lunch, are all set in the long-term memory.

Even if our brain has a very useful maintenance mechanism, called *"forgetting"*, by applying very simple memory techniques, we can strengthen our memories even from the learning phase.

Since memories are a series of nerve pathways and connections that are either successfully made and each memory has a unique trace, formed from connections between neurons in our brains, the strength of that trace determines the strength of the memory. The role of memory techniques is to create more powerful connections and thus, to strengthen the trace.

When we want to learn something, it is long-term memories we are interested in. But, how are they formed? And how can we strengthen our memories by applying the memorization techniques?

The first step of the memorization process is **Observation.** The senses are the brain's link with the environment. Through the five senses of sight, smell, hearing, touch, and taste, the brain constantly receives information from the external environment.

Although all the 5 senses are exposed to a large amount of raw information, only some of them transform into mental images, and these are the **ones to whom we pay attention.** Attention is the one that clarifies in detail the images, so that they can be processed by the brain. The purpose of Attention is getting a clear mental picture of what is seen, with all its details, by focus and fixing the object because the human brain thinks in pictures, who are the brain's alphabet.

This is the moment when the brain collects the information and creates memories. From this moment starts the memorization process. If at this moment, we apply an effective memory system, the remembering process will be much easier.

Interest plays an essential role in the maintaining of attention. Your memory in a particular area is directly proportional to the interest you have in it.

Besides interest, **Comprehension,** and **Previous Knowledge about the subject** also play an important role in maintaining attention. The more deeply you grasp what you observe, the more easily and the more in detail it will remain in your memory. The more you know on a certain subject, the more easily you can memorize everything new about it.

The SCALM technique, as a proactive learning process, is organized around these laws of memory, and for this reason it is very effective.

Let's see how these laws are integrated into the SCALM method:

The first step of this method is to **structure the information**. When you learn new material, the goal of the observation process is to see the full picture of the subject, to get a very basic understanding of how all the parts fit together.

According to *"the law of previous knowledge"* I mentioned earlier, if you already have a structure of knowledge on which to hang the new information, you can keep the parts in context and you process the information in a way your mind knows how to manage.

The next step of the method, **chunking,** is a consequence of the natural limitations that our memory has. Since there are limits on the amount of information that people can hold in short-term memory, this type of memory is enhanced when people can chunk information into familiar patterns.

Top learners and memory experts are more likely to organize any new material they have to recall into organized and meaningful chunks of information. Their superior recall ability has been explained by scientists in terms of how they "*chunk*" various elements of material into easy-to-handle pieces by the brain. Based on these chunks, they create a well-organized mental structure of knowledge around the studied material.

The third stage of the method, the **Association**, is the key to any efficient memorization.

The secret of a trained memory is the conscious and controlled associations. A super-learner knows how to consciously create his mental associations so that his mental images are extremely memorable.

But, to create unforgettable images in our brains, we must apply some memory techniques that will help us transform the things we want to remember (concepts, topics, foreign words, numbers, dates, names, and so on) into easy-to-remember images. To memorize abstract notions, these must be reduced to simple and concrete images like objects, animals, or persons. For example, when you learn abstract concepts like "concerning government" and "financial matters", you can reduce these general terms to simple symbols like – *"a crown"* and *"a coin"* respectively.

The next step is to place these images along mental routes (**Localization**), using the Memory Palace Technique. This is another application of the *"memory law of previous knowledge."*

The scientists have discovered that, when the memory athletes memorize information, they use the region in their brains, the hippocampus, that is especially important for spatial memory. This means that super-learners use a "spatial learning strategy", and, for them, learning is essentially a mental journey among concepts placed in a predetermined order.

This extremely powerful ancient technique uses known routes from your life to create an imaginary mnemonic structure that will help you memorize any list of items, by forming associations between the items to be memorized and the places where you put them. The most common type of memory palace involves making a journey through a place you know well, like a building or town. You associate all the images you want to learn with the places and combine them into one image. The weirdness of the associations between the mnemonic images and the places where you hang them will help you to memorize better. By practicing this method, you will usually work with weird mental images such as *"a crocodile swimming in your bathtub"* or "*a dinosaur laying down in the station where you wait for the subway in the morning"*, but weirdness and absurd are normal parts of an efficient memorization process.

The final step of the SCALM technique is **Memorization**, when you rehearse the learned material in your mind, by walking again mentally along your routes.

The ultimate test of learning is the process of recall, meaning that you should be able to recall the learned information, exactly as and when it is required. By using the 5 steps of the SCALM technique, instead of making random memorization, you will learn in a proactive and organized way and you will be able to recall the firmly memorized information.

As you could see in this chapter, the SCALM method follows the natural learning path of the brain, and, to learn effectively, we must follow these 5 steps:

Structure- **C**hunk- **A**ssociate- **L**ocate-**M**emorize (S.C.A.L.M.)

In the next chapter, we will discuss the types of materials we have to learn in our studies, which will help us choose the most suitable memory techniques for our learning.

Chapter Four: What We Learn

The purpose of this chapter is to emphasize the diversity that exists among the materials we need to learn in our studies or our careers.

The biology lessons we dealt with in school, for example, are quite different from the many types of materials that we need to learn for our jobs, whether they are public speaking scripts or different procedures that we have to apply in our work. However, regardless of the type of material you want to learn, the approach of the SCALM method is the same, because any type material can be reduced to a series of more or less complex concepts, which this technique treats similar, regardless of whether they are notions of astronomy or medieval art.

The bricks that make up any learning material are the concepts, placed in a certain order, to ensure the presentation logic.

Let's see the types of concepts any learning material can contain.

First of all, there are **concrete (perceptual) concepts**. These concepts can easily be associated with images of objects, animals, or people since they naturally create a concrete image in the brain. When you read the word "dog" in a text, your mind creates the image of a dog. Usually, if it's a generic term, your brain will create the image of a certain dog that is familiar to you.

Concrete concepts are the easiest to memorize. You just have to put them in context (in a place from your memory palace), and you will remember them for a long time.

Then, there are **abstract concepts** like numbers, dates, mathematical formulas, or **abstract notions** like freedom or integrity.

Why is it so difficult to remember numbers and other abstract notions? Because they do not have a meaning for the brain. If we can do something to give some kind of meaning to these abstract concepts and can conjure up a mental image of them, learning would be easier. Also, you cannot visualize abstract concepts. And if you cannot visualize, it is difficult to remember.

The trick here is to transform them into some images of objects, animals, or people, real things that can be pictured in your mind.

For example, for the word *"freedom",* you can associate the image of the Statue of Liberty. In this way, the abstract concept will become easier to memorize.

The last type of concept we encounter in the texts we have to learn is **complex concepts** like schemas, scripts, or classifications.

- A *schema* is a drawing that represents an idea or theory and makes it easier to understand;
- A *script*, on the other hand, is a set of instructions that a person follows to complete he desired goal. An example of a script would be how *to use a new technical device, like a phone or a TV set.* Several actions must occur before the actual act of using that device and a script provides you with the necessary actions and proper order of these actions to be successful.

- A *classification* is a systematic list of ideas or items, which help us to recognize, differentiate, and understand them in context.

We should ask ourselves the question: what should be our learning strategy when we face such complex concepts?

The answer is that no such concept can be learned until it is somehow transformed through deconstructing, organizing, and reconstructing, and this is what the SCALM method does.

By using a mix of very efficient memory techniques, the method aims to transform abstract and cumbersome information into easy-to-remember images.

So, we have concrete concepts that can be directly associated with memorable images, we have abstract concepts that we must consciously associate with memorable images that we deliberately choose, and we have these complex concepts that we must process before transforming them into easy-to-learn images.

In the next chapter, you will learn what are the memory techniques used by the SCALM method are and how they work.

Chapter Five: Overview of the Memory Techniques

In this chapter, you will learn about the memory techniques used by the SCALM method to transform abstract information into easy to memorize images.

For now, I will just give you an overview of them, but in the following chapters you'll see in detail how these techniques work in practice.

MEMORY TECHNIQUES OVERVIEW

Step	Memory Techniques Used
1. **Structure**	• Mind maps
2. **Chunk**	• Simplification • Symbolization
3. **Associate**	• Acronyms and The Sentence Method • The Story Method • The Sound Alike Technique • Rhymes and Jingles • The Names Association Technique • The Major System
4. **Locate**	• Memory Palace Technique
5. **Memorize**	• Review • Rehearse

The first step of the SCALM method is to **Structure the information**, to get the full picture of the subject and a very basic understanding of how all the parts fit together.

For this purpose, the method uses a highly efficient tool called "Mind Maps".

Sometimes, the material we have to learn is already organized by the author in the form of charts, diagrams, or lists that give us an overview of the information contained therein. But, most of the time, we have to build on our own overview, which will help us throughout our learning process, and Mind Maps are excellent tools for this purpose.

Invented by the memory Expert and founder of the World Memory Championships Tony Buzan, Mind maps are one of the best logical organization tools.

A *"Mind map"* is a one-page hierarchical diagram representing ideas, concepts, and words that are arranged around a central image or key idea.

It is a creative and effective tool, which literally 'maps out' the subject you have to learn, by piecing it into effective segments or chunks to help aid memory and recall.

The next step of the SCALM method is to **chunk the material** into organized and meaningful pieces of information.

You probably heard a lot of times by now the question: *"How Do You Eat an Elephant?"*There is only one way to eat an elephant: a bite at a time.

In the same way, your memory will improve if you feed it with little chunks of information instead of a continuous flow of mixed information.

The two memory principles used in this stage are *Simplification* and *Symbolization.*

- *Simplification* means distilling complex ideas into simple mental images that are quickly understood;

- *Symbolization* means the association of abstract concepts, for which the brain has no concrete representation (such as the notion of *"freedom"*), with concrete and easy-to-remember images of people, objects, or animals.

The next step is the **Association**. This is where the magic happens. At this stage, each piece of information is transformed into memorable images, by applying memory techniques.

The secret of a trained memory is the conscious and controlled associations. A top learner knows how to consciously create his mental associations so that the created mental images are extremely memorable.

From this moment on, to create unforgettable memories in our brains, we must apply some tested memory techniques.

Here are the memory techniques that help you transform the things you want to remember (concepts, topics, foreign words, numbers, dates, names, and so on), into easy-to-remember images:

- Acronyms and The Sentence Method
- The Story Method
- The Sound-Alike Technique

- Rhymes and Jingles
- The Names Association Technique
- The Major System

Please note that there are two types of memory techniques:

1. **Encoding memory techniques** that transform the things you want to remember into easy to recall images. All the techniques used in the association stage are of this type.

Every item becomes an image that you will place along the mnemonic structure created with the structural techniques, which will give you the order.

2. **Structural memory techniques**, that help you create a structure for your mental images (like *"The Memory Palace Method"* and *"The Peg System"*).This type of techniques are used in the next step of the SCALM Method.

The next step is to **place the images created with the encoding techniques along with mental structures**, by using the *Memory Palace Technique*. This extremely powerful technique uses known routes from your life to create an imaginary mnemonic structure, which will help you memorize any list of items, by forming associations between the items and the places where you put them.

A Memory Palace is an imaginary structure that you consciously create in your mind, to place your mnemonic images there. Despite its name, a memory palace does not necessarily have to be a building. It can be a mental journey through well-known places like your daily route to school or the route to visit a friend. Along that mental journey; there are specific locations that you use to visit in the same order. To memorize your images created in the previous step of the SCALM method, you them with the route markers and combine them into one image. The weirdness of the associations between your mnemonic images and the places where you hang them will help you memorize them better.

The final step of the method is the **Memorization** of the re-organized information. After you have already gone through the previous steps of the method, now you only have to learn some series of easy-to-remember images.

Two easy memory techniques, *Review,* and *Rehearsal* can help you solidify the memories in your mind.

- In *Review*, you go over what you have just learned to more firmly encode it in the first place;

- In *Rehearsal,* you expand on your initial review with a return to the material, so you firmly fix that encoding in place by visualization ("mentally rehearsing"), by mentally walking in your memory palace.

So, we have a set of memory techniques that we can use in our learning process. Further in this book, you will learn how each of them works and how to choose them according to the type of information you have to learn.

Now you're set up and ready to learn in detail each step of this highly efficient technique, so I'll see you in the next part of this book.

PART III: The 5 Steps of the SCALM Method

Chapter Six: Step 1.Structure the Information

In this part, I will present in detail every step of the method, along with a practical example that we will continue throughout several chapters, so that you can better understand how it works.

The first step of the SCALM method is to **Structure the learning material**. After you know how the information is structured, you will get the full picture of the subject and you will understand how the parts fit together. This way, you can keep the parts in context and you are able to process the information in a way your mind knows how to manage.

In the same way that a building has a structure, each learning material must have a structure or framework around which information is organized and you will be much more effective if you start your learning by observing this structure.

But, how to approach the structuring of any type of information, given the diversity of materials that we have to learn throughout our lives? Is there a universal method that can be used to structure any type of information?

There are cases where the material is already organized by the author in the form of tables, charts, lists, or tables of contents. We can use these as an overview of the information, but only if they are organized in a visual form. Unfortunately, these cases are quite rare, so we need a universal instrument that can be applied to any type of material.

For this purpose, the SCALM technique often uses a very efficient tool, known as "*Mind Maps*", also used by millions of people around the world to organize their ideas and to think more creatively.

A *Mind map* is a diagram used to visually organize information, by showing the relationships between ideas. The theme is at the center, and the ideas that follow from that core idea are clustered around it.

You can summarize a whole book in a one-page diagram, which makes mind maps a great tool for the first step of the SCALM method.

Originated in the late 1960s by Tony Buzan, a British psychologist and author of several books on the subject of learning and memorizing, Mind Maps uses imagery, drawings, and color to structure a specific subject or material so that it becomes as memorable as possible for the brain. Because the information is visual, it's easier to picture it in your mind's eye.

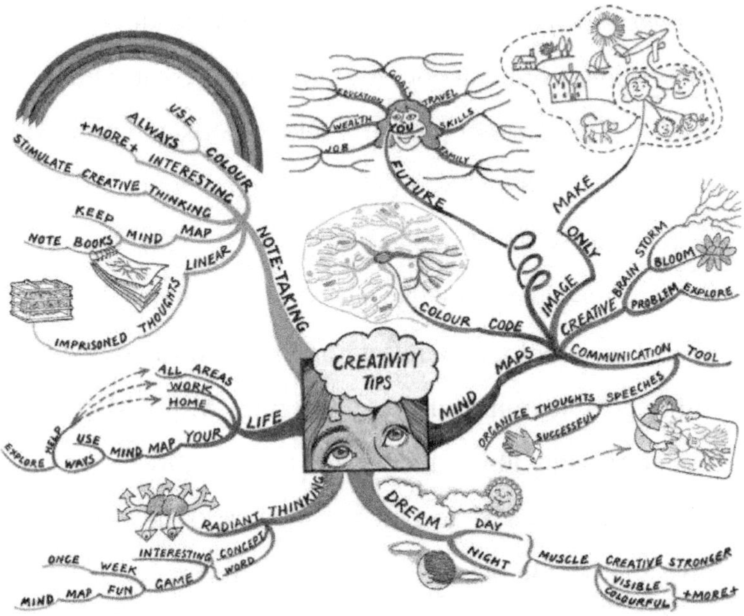

Source: *"The Ultimate Book of Mind Maps"*- by Tony Buzan

According to its creator: *"You can compare a Mind Map to a map of a city. The center of your Mind Map is like the center of the city. It represents your most important idea. The main roads leading from the center represent the main thoughts in your thinking process; the secondary roads represent your secondary thoughts, and so on. Special images or shapes can represent sites of interest or particularly interesting ideas."*

As Tony Buzan explains in his book *"The Ultimate Book of Mind Maps"*, there are 7 rules you must follow when creating a mind map:

"1. Start in the CENTRE of a blank page turned sideways.

Why? Because starting in the center gives your Brain freedom to spread out in all directions and to express itself more freely and naturally.

2. Use an IMAGE or PICTURE for your central idea.

Why? Because an image is worth a thousand words and helps you use your Imagination. A central image is more interesting, keeps you focused, helps you concentrate, and gives your brain more of a buzz!

3. Use COLOURS throughout.

Why? Because colours are as exciting to your Brain as are images. Colour adds extra vibrancy and life to your Mind Map, adds tremendous energy to your Creative Thinking, and is fun!

4. CONNECT your MAIN BRANCHES to the central image and connect your second- and third-level branches to the first and second levels, etc.

Why? Because your brain works by association. It likes to link two (or three, or four) things together. If you connect the branches, you will understand and remember a lot more easily. Connecting your main branches also creates and establishes a basic structure or architecture for your thoughts. This is very similar to the way in which in nature a tree has connected branches that radiate from its central trunk. If there were little gaps between the trunk and its main branches or between those main branches and the smaller branches and twigs, nature wouldn't work quite so well! Without connection in your Mind Map, everything (especially your memory and learning!) falls apart. Connect!

5. Make your branches CURVED rather than straight-lined.

Why? Because having nothing but straight lines are boring to your brain. Curved, organic branches, like the branches of trees, are far more attractive and riveting to your eye.

6. Use ONE KEY WORD PER LINE.

Why? Because single key words give your Mind Map more power and flexibility. Every single word or image is like a multiplier, generating its special array of associations and connections. When you use single keywords, each one is freer and therefore better able to spark off new ideas and new thoughts. Phrases or sentences tend to dampen this triggering effect. A Mind Map with more keywords in it is like a hand with all the finger joints working. A Mind Map with phrases or sentences is like a hand with all your fingers held in rigid splints!

7. Use IMAGES throughout.

Why? Because each image, like the central image, is also worth a thousand words. So if you have only 10 images in your Mind Map, it's already the equal of 10,000 words of notes!"

Therefore, a Mind Map gives us an overview of the information structure. We do not have to go into too much detail, because the purpose of this stage is just to give us a general picture of how the chapters and ideas are organized.

Usually, one branch from the mind map is assigned for each chapter, and for the main ideas sub-branches are allocated. I recommend you to use different colors for each branch since for each branch you will later create a distinct mental journey to memorize that paragraph or chapter.

When the material is very wide, such as if you have to learn a whole book, your mind map can become quite large and you may need to create a mind map for each chapter.

Now, let's take an example that will continue in future lessons, following the steps of the SCALM method.

Let's learn this historical essay, extracted from the book *"History of the Catholic Church from the Renaissance to the French Revolution - Volume 1"* by James MacCaffrey:

"Risings of the peasantry took place in various parts of Germany, notably in Swabia, Thuringia, the Rhine Provinces, and Saxony (1524). Thomas Munzer, the leader of the Anabaptists, encouraged them in their fight for freedom. At first the attack was directed principally against the spiritual princes. Many monasteries and churches were plundered, and several of the nobles were put to death. Soon the lay princes of Germany, alarmed by the course of the revolutionaries and fearing for the safety of their own territories, assembled their forces and marched against the insurgents. The war was carried on mercilessly on both sides, close upon 100,000 peasants being killed in the field, while many of their leaders, amongst them Thomas Munzer, were arrested and condemned to death. In nearly every important engagement the peasants, as might be expected, suffered defeat, so that before the end of 1525 the movement was, practically speaking, at an end. Luther, who had been consulted by both sides, and who had tried to avoid committing himself to either, frightened by the very violence of the storm he had been

instrumental in creating, issued an appeal to the princes calling upon them to show no mercy to the forces of disorder, and even Melanchthon, gentle and moderate as he usually was, did not hesitate to declare that the peasants of Germany had more liberty than should be allowed to such a rude and uncultured people. The Peasants' War, disastrous as it was, did some good by opening men's eyes to the dangerous consequences of Luther's extravagant harangues, and by giving some slight indications as to the real character and methods of the man, who was posing as a heaven-sent reformer and at the same time as a champion of popular liberty."

Like most history essays, it combines ideas, data, and names quite difficult to remember, and for this reason I think it is a very good example to show you how the SCALM method works.

The first step of the SCALM technique is to create a short mind map containing the main ideas from this text. I have extracted these main ideas, which give me an overview of the structure of the text, as follows:

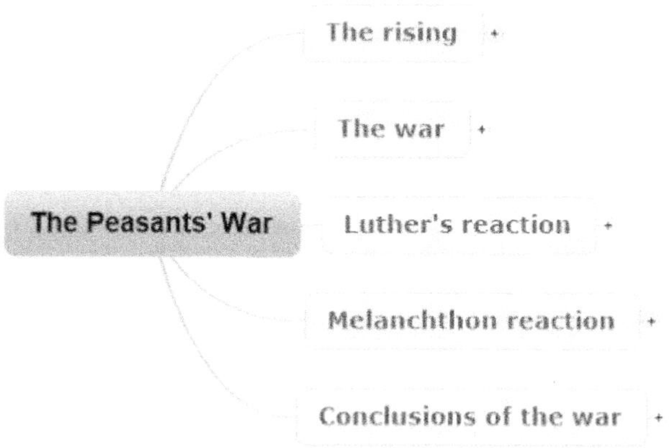

I have to tell you that, for this mind map, I used a mind mapping software, but most of the time it is recommended to draw your map by hand, using colored pencils.

As you can see, the main advantage of a mind map is that all the information is on one page, so it's possible to take it in all at once and to picture it in your mind's eye. You can summarize a whole book on a one-page mind map, which makes it a great tool for learning.

With this mind map, the first step of the SCALM method is made. In the next chapter, after I explain to you how the second step works, we will continue this example.

I'll see you in the next chapter, to talk about chunking the information into easy-to-manipulate pieces.

Chapter Seven: Step 2. Chunking the Material

The second stage of the SCALM method is **Chunking**, a process by which the material is broken down into organized and meaningful pieces of information.

To make learning faster and easier, chunking is one of the most effective memory strategies. Almost everything of what we have to learn can easily turn into a list, by splitting the concepts up into small pieces or "chunks" of information.

Super-learners prepare any new material they need to recall, by splitting it into organized and significant chunks of data. Based on these chunks, they produce a well-organized mental structure of information around the studied material.

A chunk is a set of 2 to 7 of familiar items that have been grouped for the purpose of being stored in a person's memory. The chunks can be retrieved more easily due to their simplicity and familiarity. Breaking down or arranging the information into a simple pattern is the first step toward organizing it.

So, having an overview of the material that we obtained in the first stage with the help of a mind map, we now begin to chunk it into pieces that we will later associate with images that can be easily memorized.

The chunking process can be highly subjective because it is based on personal perceptions and past experiences, which can be linked to the information set.

Two memory mechanisms make the chunking process more efficient and these are *Simplification* and *Symbolization.*

1. Simplification means distilling complex ideas into simple mental images that are quickly understood.

Let's assume you have to learn a larger medical material that contains the following list of medical terms:

Causes of Atrial Fibrillation

- **P**ulmonary embolism,
- **I**schemic heart disease,

- **R**heumatic valvular disease
- **A**nemia
- **T**hyroid disease
- **E**levated blood pressure (hypertension)
- **S**epsis

This list is only a chunk from the larger material, but we can simplify it by creating an acronym that will help us to memorize all these items in order: "**PIRATES**", a simple and concrete image that can be easily memorized.

We often underestimate the simplification required for an efficient learning process. If you get in the habit of simplifying things before you memorize them, it will be easier for you to remember them later.

2. Symbolization means the association of abstract concepts, for which the brain has no concrete representation, such as the notion of *"freedom"*, with concrete and easy-to-remember images of people, objects, or animals. Symbolization also forces you to simplify.

Instead of dealing with abstracts, you now have to deal with images of real things, and these images are your brain's alphabet. Instead of using the concept of *"love"*, for example, perhaps you will symbolize it by using "*a heart*".

Your brain makes fewer connections when you juggle ideas only at an abstract level, so try to make more tangible connections and you will remember more.

At the end of the chunking stage of the SCALM method, the learning material will become a list of items, which will be associated in the next stage with memorable images, created with the help of the memory techniques.

Now that you know how chunking works, let's continue our example from the previous chapter by chunking the material into manageable pieces.

Here is how our essay will look like:

1.Rising
Risings of the peasantry took place in various parts of Germany, notably in Swabia, Thuringia, the Rhine Provinces, and Saxony (1524).
Thomas Munzer, the leader of the Anabaptists, encouraged them in their fight for freedom.
At first the attack was directed principally against the spiritual princes. Many monasteries and churches were plundered, and several of the nobles were put to death.

Soon the lay princes of Germany, alarmed by the course of the revolutionaries and fearing for the safety of their own territories, assembled their forces and marched against the insurgents.
2.The War
The war was carried on mercilessly on both sides, close upon 100,000 peasants being killed in the field, while many of their leaders, amongst them Thomas Munzer, were arrested and condemned to death.
In nearly every important engagement the peasants, as might be expected, suffered defeat, so that before the end of 1525 the movement was, practically speaking, at an end.
3.Luther's reaction
Luther, who had been consulted by both sides, and who had tried to avoid committing himself to either, frightened by the very violence of the storm he had been instrumental in creating, issued an appeal to the princes calling upon them to show no mercy to the forces of disorder,
4.Melanchthon's reaction
and even Melanchthon, gentle and moderate as he usually was, did not hesitate to declare that the peasants of Germany had more liberty than should be allowed to such rude and uncultured people.
5.Conclusions of the war
The Peasants' War, disastrous as it was, did some good by opening men's eyes to the dangerous consequences of Luther's extravagant harangues,
and by giving some slight indications as to the real character and methods of the man, who was posing as a heaven-sent reformer and at the same time as a champion of popular liberty.

I tried to make these pieces as simple as possible, to be symbolized by images as relevant as possible. Of course, this is a fairly small text, but when learning longer texts, a more general symbolization, that allows cutting larger chunks, will be needed.

With this, the second step of the method is completed.

In the following chapters, after you learn how memory techniques work, we will continue this example and I will teach you how to convert these chunks into memorable images.

Chapter Eight: Step 3.Association

We typically remember one thing because we are reminded of it by another thing.

This association, or *"vinculis"* in Latin, has its roots in the ancient art of magic. In the Middle Ages, scientists wrote entire volumes about it.

The great philosopher and scientist Aristotle, who developed the first scientific approach to studying memory, believed that memories are like some thumbnails of the real things. The brain stores and processes these thumbnails, these are the alphabet with which it works. When it comes to remembering, these thumbnails are functioning as shortcuts to the real things.

But, what if we could choose the thumbnails to store in our memory? What if we could learn to work directly with the brain alphabet, made up exclusively of images stored in our memory?

Here is a key principle in learning: *To remember any newly learned concept, it must be associated with something we already know or already remember.*

And for this, we must resort to the most efficient mechanism that our memory has incorporated into it: **Association.**

Association means linking together of two "things" and create a hook, through which one of them will bring to light the other from the depths of memory. The association can be made only between two things(and no more). One of these things is already known and is easy to remember. It will trigger the memory of the other thing, which is new for the brain. After recording this association in memory, the brain will think about those two things in an associative way.

Association is the key mechanism on which all memory techniques are based. But, for the purpose of efficient learning, the association needs to be a **conscious and controlled process.**

By choosing to be your mental movie director and to filter the images recorded by your brain, you take control of the way your memory store the information.

From the perspective of our memory, an efficient association is an association that cannot be easily forgotten, and this can be done by applying a few tips and tricks which aim to exaggerate the images to make them as memorable as possible.

As memory expert Harry Lorraine wrote:

"We tend to forget the simple, mundane, everyday, ordinary things. We rarely forget the unique, the violent, the unusual, the absurd, the extraordinary. Make your associations unusual, ridiculous, and impossible—and they'll stick like burrs"

German psychologist Hedwig von Restorff identified, in 1933, a very interesting memory phenomenon, known as "*the Von Restorff effect*", according to which: "*things that stand out from their peers are more memorable*". In other words, an object that is notably different from the rest in size, color, or other basic characteristics will be more readily recalled than the others, because the attention is usually captured by salient, novel, surprising, or distinctive stimuli.

Being different is not better or worse, but different is memorable!

Therefore, if you want to remember something better, make it stand out! You can be very creative in making your associations more memorable and here are the tools that you can use for this purpose:

1. Involve all your senses in your mental image

Besides the sight, try to include tasting, touching, smelling, and hearing when you create your mental image. Think about rhyme in words, sounds objects might make or what smell they have. Combine as many of these features as possible, in unique and unusual ways. The more details you add, the more triggers you have to remind you of that image later.

2. Use exaggeration!

For some reason, our memory loves exaggeration. Apply Harry Lorraine's *"Slap in the face" principle*:

> *"If you walked out of your office and a few drops of rain splattered on to you, you would quickly forget it ever happened. If, however, buckets of water poured over your head, soaking you—you would remember the event and probably recount it in detail for years"*

Exaggerate situations by using unusual circumstances!

Let us say you are reading a book about monkeys. After reading a few pages, if a real monkey jumps out of the book, I am sure you will never forget that ever!

Exaggerate the proportion!

You've probably heard by now that size does matter and that big things create a big impact. If you try to remember, for example, that you have to buy dog food, and you have in mind the image of a huge,3 meters tall, dog barking at you in the supermarket, you probably won't forget what you have to buy.

3. Create impact images by using Color and Motion

Color and moving things attract, and whatever attracts the brain is remembered with ease and for a long time. For example, imagine that you are at the airport. There are two planes on the runways. One is standing still. The other one is just taking off. Which one gains your attention? Undoubtedly, is it not the moving one?

You can make things more memorable by making them interacting, by crashing or sticking them together, by putting them on top or inside each other, or by placing them in new situations.

4. Keep them simple!

Only use objects and features involved in the association you're making and avoid involving unrelated objects which can distract you.

Remember that association is about only two things (and no more), of which one will act as a memory trigger for the other. This trigger must be as simple and concrete as possible, without needing mental juggling only to get it.

5. Put yourself in the story!

As eight-time World Memory Champion Dominic O'Brien wrote:

"You will remember more information if you try to relate that information to yourself. By putting yourself in the story created from mnemonic images, you somehow trick your brain into believing that the experience has happened to you"

Memory techniques are the ones that help us transform the chunks into easy-to-remember images.

Here is an overview of memory techniques used by SCALM method in the association stage:

1. Acronyms and The Sentence Method
2. The Story Method
3. The Sound-Alike Technique
4. Rhymes and Jingles
5. The Names Association Technique
6. The Major System

As you will see in the following pages, in which I will present each of these techniques, they are very simple to learn and easy to apply.

Memory Technique #1: Acronyms and The Sentence Method

What is an Acronym?

According to Wikipedia, *"an Acronym is a word or name formed from the initial components of a longer name or phrase, usually using individual initial letters, as in NATO (North Atlantic Treaty Organization) or EU (European Union), but sometimes using syllables, as in Benelux (Belgium, Netherlands, and Luxembourg), or a mixture of the two, as in radar (Radio Detection And Ranging). Similarly, acronyms are sometimes pronounced as words, as in NASA or UNESCO, sometimes as the individual letters, as in FBI or ATM, or a mixture of the two, as in JPEG or IUPAC."*

The new word formed by an acronym is easier to write and say than the sum of its parts. For this reason, acronyms are increasingly used today in all languages, is one of how the vocabulary of a language increases with new words

You probably are familiar with many of the acronyms that are in common use, such as :

- SONAR, created from ***so****und* ***na****vigation and* ***r****anging,* or

- SCUBA: for **s**elf-**c**ontained **u**nderwater **b**reathing **a**pparatus

Besides their role of shortening different expressions, acronyms can be used successfully to help us memorize different things, especially when they are in sequential list form.

The Acronym Mnemonic Technique is very simple to learn and to apply and can be used both in the study and in different daily activities.

This technique has two variants:

- **The Acronym Method** and
- **The Sentence Method**.

The first method uses a single word formed from the initials of the items in the list, while the second method creates a mnemonic phrase formed of words beginning with these initials.

Let's view how each method works:

A. THE ACRONYM METHOD

You may be familiar with some acronyms used to help you remember items in school, such as :

• **The Colors of the Rainbow**(red, orange, yellow, green, blue, indigo, violet) can be memorized with the acronym "ROY G. BIV", while

• **The Great Lakes** (Huron, Ontario, Michigan, Erie, and Superior) are memorized with the acronym "HOMES".

Here is how you can use this method as a memory technique:

Take the first letter of each word in a set you want to remember and create a word using those letters. Then, you use that word to trigger your memory for every word in the set. Hearing the first letter of each word helps you recall the whole word you want to remember.

Here are the 3 steps of the technique:

1. Write the concepts you need to memorize one below other, in the form of a list.

2. Underline the first letter of each concept. If there is more than one word in a concept, underline the first letter of only the first word.

3. Arrange the underlined letters to form an acronym. This can be a real word or a nonsense word you can easily pronounce.

For example, here is a checklist a pilot might use before lining up on the runway:

- **F**laps Set, Fuel Pump On.
- **I**nstruments Checked and Set.
- **S**witches set.
- **T**ransponder set to ALT.

This list can be memorized by using the acronym: "FIST"

Sometimes, an acronym uses a second letter from a word in the series, most commonly a vowel, to make the acronym easier to read and often a small word like "of" or ''and'' is dropped in creating the acronym, like in FBI for the *Federal Bureau ~~of~~ Investigation.*

Applications of the Acronym method

a) The most common application of the Acronym Method is **Memorizing lists of things.**

Whether you are a student or you need to memorize material for your work, learning how to memorize lists is a great way to improve your learning.

As I have already shown in the chapter on chunking, almost everything of what we have to learn can easily turn into a list, by splitting the concepts up into small "chunks" of information. It is undeniable that chunking is one of the most effective learning strategies. However, even after we turned the information into a list, it is still difficult to memorize the exact order of the items on the list. But, Acronyms can help you making lists manageable.

Let's practice putting some acronyms together. Assume you had to memorize some of the following ideas in school:

- The 5 layers of the human scalp (Skin, Connective tissue, Aponeurosis epicranial, Loose areolar tissue, Pericranium) can be memorized with the acronym "*SCALP*"

- The stages of cell division (Interphase, Prophase, Metaphase, Anaphase, Telophase) can be memorized with the acronym *"IPMAT"*. Notice that, in this example, you cannot form a real word using the first letter of each fact to be remembered, but the Acronym "IPMAT" can be easily pronounced and memorized.

- Here is another Acronym:" *SOH-CAH-TOA"* is a mnemonic device that is used in mathematics to remember the definitions of the three most common trigonometric functions.

- SOH Sine – opposite times hypotenuse
- COH Cosine –opposite times hypotenuse
- TOA Tangent –opposite times adjacent

If you have a particularly long list to remember, you can use more than one acronym. Break the list down into groups(by type, color or shape, and so on), then create an acronym for each group.

b) Using Acronyms in daily life

You can create your acronym to help you remember a shortlist of items or tasks to do.

- **"CAT"** will help you memorize the following products: **C**arrots, **A**pricots, **T**omatoes.

- **"EAR"** will remind you of **E**ggplant, **A**pples, and **R**adish.

Here is a 10 items grocery list, in alphabetical order that we can easily memorize with the Acronym

Technique: *Apples, Avocados, Bananas, Bread, Butter, Cheese, Eggplant, Garlic, Grapefruit, Ice Cream.*

By rearranging the first letters, we get the words: "**BIG CABBAGE**". This mnemonic acronym will trigger your memory for every word in the set.

c) Using Acronyms in your Career

Acronyms can also be used to design a memorable speech or presentation.

Here is how it works:

Take a word that is relevant to your speech and important to the audience and use it as an acronym, by creating a structure of concepts, each starting with a letter of this word.

For example, you can take the word SUCCESS and create a list of 7 success factors, like in this example:

- Sense of direction;
- Understanding;

- Courage;
- Charity;
- Esteem;
- Self-confidence;
- Self-acceptance.

By elaborating on each factor, you will able to speak without notes for 30 minutes to 1 hour and never lose your place. You can do this with almost any word, whether it's a three-letter word or a 10-letter word. This method is an effective way to organize your key ideas and to impress your audience by speaking fluently without notes.

B. THE SENTENCE METHOD

The Sentence Method is very similar to the Acronym Method.

In the same way that we remember a list by forming an Acronym, we can create sentences to remember useful pieces of information.

Here is how The Sentence Method works:

You take the first letter (or an important letter) of the word you're trying to memorize and form a sentence out of it. The first letters of the words in the sentence reminds us of what we want to recall because they are the same as the first letters of the words in the list. Each first letter is a clue to an item from the list you need to remember.

This method is better for longer lists as compared to *the Acronym Method* because a sentence allows you to create much more elaborate mnemonic images than a single word.

The Sentence Method is particularly helpful when you have to memorize things in a particular order because the logic of the phrase will help you remember the order of the items.

Here is how to form an Acronymic Sentence (also known as an "Acrostic"), when you have to memorize facts or concepts:

1. Write the concepts you need to remember.
2. Underline the first letter of each concept. If there is more than one word in the concept, underline the first letter of only the first word.
3. Arrange the underlined letters to form a memorable sentence.

Here are the two examples presented earlier, which we can now memorize by using the sentence method:

• **The colors of the rainbow**: *"Richard Of York Goes Battling In Vain"*

• **The Great Lakes:** *"Sergeant Major Hates Eating Onions"*

Applications of the Sentence Method

a) Remember Lists

As with the Acronym method, the most important use of the sentence method is to memorize lists of items. Almost everything of what you have to learn can ultimately be reduced to an ordered list of items, so it is important to know how to apply this method.

Assume you had to memorize some of the following items in school:

- The countries of Central America, in order from North America to South America: Guatemala, Belize, Honduras, El Salvador, Nicaragua, Costa Rica, Panama-

Think of the phrase: "*Green bananas help sister nations create prosperity*".

- The names of the nine muses in Greek mythology: Calliope, Clio, Erato, Terpsichore, Euterpe, Melpomene, Thalia, Polymnia, Urania.

You might think of the phrase: *"Count Clambering Elephants Thundering Eastward, Mighty Trunks Pointing Up".*

- **The signs of the zodiac** - Aries, Taurus, Gemini, Cancer, Leo, Virgo, Libra, Scorpio, Sagittarius, Capricorn, Aquarius, Pisces.

Think of the phrase: "*A Tall Giraffe Chewed Leaves Very Low, Some Slow Cows At Play.*"

- This is how some people remember **numerical prefixes**(kilo-, hecto-, deca-, metric-, deci-, centi-, and milli-):

- *"Kippers Hardly Dare Move During Cold Months",* **or**

- *"Kings Hate Dragons, Maybe Dragons Can't Make Money."*

Medical Students are famous for making up mnemonics, both acronyms and sentences. The amount of medical information they have to learn, particularly concerning human anatomy, has inevitably led to some highly ingenious mnemonics.

This one is used for remembering the nerves in the superior orbital tissue (lacrimal, frontal, trochlear, lateral, nasociliary, internal, abduction): *"Lazy French Tarts Lie Naked In Anticipation".*

b) Using The Sentence Method in daily life

You can create your phrases to help you remember a shortlist of items or tasks to do.

For example, you can memorize the grocery list presented earlier (Apples, Avocados, Bananas, Bread, Butter, Cheese, Eggplant, Garlic, Grapefruit, and Ice Cream), by using the sentence: *"Additives Attack Brilliant Barrels Because Cool Elephants Get Gorgeous Islands"*

c) Using the method in your career

Regardless of whom you are and what type of job you currently have or plan to have, there's a good chance that one day you will be required to make a presentation for your colleagues or your clients.

These two methods (Acronyms and The Sentence Method), can help you to design a memorable presentation around your mnemonic, that will help you garner the respect and support of others, in your career or your personal life.

If you are a teacher, creating and practicing these methods will help your students to organize their new knowledge, rehearse it, and eventually transfer it to long-term memory. After all, a teacher's goal is always to teach students things they'll remember from year to year.

It's also fun to create acronyms and mnemonic sentences as a whole class activity. Students might compose an acronym to aid in memorizing the parts of a flower, an insect, or a tree.

These simple methods can help you in many situations, so do not forget to use them on every occasion.

But how to recognize where to use these techniques with the SCALM Method?

Whenever we have to learn shortlists of up to 10-12 items, *Acronyms and the Sentence Method* should be our first option, being very easy to use and at the same time very efficient.

Memory Technique #2: The Story Method

The Story Method is one of the easiest mnemonic techniques available.

It works by coding information to be remembered into images and then linking these images together into a story, by creating a continuous narration, featuring them. So, you take the information to be memorized, organized in a form of o list of items, and weave a story around these concepts. When you repeat the story in your mind, following its narrative logic, you should recall all the items to be memorized in the right order, too.

A story is a very powerful vehicle for creating new memories. After all, the stories are deeply embedded in our thinking and our memory patterns from childhood.

A story has characters that interact with each other and it takes on a logic of its own, which will keep the order of the memorized items. The logical flow of the story and the strength of the images will make the sequence extremely memorable.

Let's view a simple example on how to use this method for memorizing a shopping list. Here is a shopping list that we need to memorize by using The Story Method:

- Olive Oil;
- Bananas;
- Dog food;
- Pizza ;
- Fish ;
- Bath sponge;
- Cabbage;
- Wine;
- Carrots;

- Broccoli.

Now, let's create a little story with these products:

*"Imagine yourself on a field and there is a big **olive tree** in the middle. Walking out of a door in the tree is a **banana**, one in pajamas. It's coming out of the door to feed **the dog**. To be more memorable, the dog will be oversized and red. It has a **pizza**-shape medal on its chest. This big dog just came from fishing, where it captured **a carp** and **a bath sponge.** Here is Mr. **Cabbage**, who holds a **bottle of wine** and is drunk. Next to him is Bugs Bunny, biting a **carrot** and asking him "What's up Doc? You need to take a little nap in the shade of **broccoli**!"*

When you have finished watching this fantasy, take a break, close your eyes, and run back through the mental movie you have just completed. Then, try to write down the 10 items, in order, on a piece of paper. I'm pretty sure you will remember all 10 different and unique pieces of information from this short but powerful little story!

When you've seen this story, you received already created mental pictures. But when you will apply this method on your own, you need to use your imagination for creating memorable stories. Allow your imagination to create pictures in your head, trying to generate sensory perceptions such as smells, noises, or the feeling of objects.

Besides lists, you can use The Story Method for remembering the names of people at a party or a business meeting or to memorize the topics you want to include in a presentation.

The method can also be very useful for your studies, helping you memorize with ease various unrelated things.

As an example, let's memorize ***the Characteristics of Culture*** by using the Story Method.

Here are the 5 characteristics that we have to learn in order:

1. *Culture is learned.*
2. *Culture is shared.*
3. *Culture is based on symbols.*
4. *Culture is integrated.*
5. *Culture is dynamic.*

The first step is to associate these abstract characteristics with concrete things:

- For the word "learned", I will associate the image of **"a book";**
- For "shared ", I can associate "a social network" **(Facebook)**;
- For the word "symbols", my first thought is about "sex symbols" **(e.g.Marilyn Monroe)**;
- For "integrated", I will use the image of "**an integrated circuit**" ;
- and for dynamic, I will associate the image of "**a marathon runner**".

Now, I have 5 images (book, Facebook, Marilyn Monroe, integrated circuit, and marathon runner), around which I need to weave a little story:

"*I can imagine that I get home and in front of my door I find a big (oversized) red book (to be more memorable). I 'm extremely surprised and I photograph it with the phone, and then share it on Facebook. After that, I receive a message from Marilyn Monroe, who writes to me that a secret integrated circuit is hidden in the book.*

As I was reading the message, a marathon runner ran past me and stole the book."

It looks like a little silly story, doesn't it? But these images are extremely memorable, which means that they will reach the goal of acting as memory triggers when we have to remember the characteristics of the culture. As long as your images are clear, there is no way you can make a mistake. You will remember the list for days, even if you don't practice it. And, because the images are what you make them, *The Story Method* can be used an infinite number of times, for any number of different lists.

Here is a tip from the eight times World Memory Champion Dominic O'Brien about this technique:

> *"Using the first person is important here. By putting yourself in the story, you somehow trick your brain into believing that the experience has happened to you. If you are part of the story, you will have feelings and emotions attached to what happens."*

As you have already seen, The Story Method is very simple to learn and to use.

Another advantage is that you can combine it with other memory techniques, as you will see later in this book.

But, how to recognize where to use this technique with the SCALM Method?

Whenever you have to memorize lists from which you cannot make an Acronym or a Mnemonic phrase, or for longer lists, The Story Method is appropriate.

Memory Technique #3: The Sound-Alike Method

The Sound-Alike Method, also known as **The Word Substitution Method**, is one of my favorite memory techniques because it is so simple, but at the same time so powerful and versatile. It is the most appropriate technique for learning new words, regardless of whether they are difficult words in your native language or foreign words that you aren't familiar with.

Unfamiliar words like the Latin names and terms that you so frequently come across in subjects like biology, medical sciences, and law, the names of places you have to remember in geography, foreign language words, etc, do offer a lot of difficulties when you try to memorize them.

But why is it so difficult to remember these strange words? The simple answer is: because they do not have a meaning for your brain. When you read or heard the word "APPLE", your mind creates the image of *an apple*. This mental image helps you in remembering the word without any difficulty.

But, in the case of an unknown word or a foreign language word, there is no previous mental image, so you have to decide in advance what the mental image should look like. Therefore, you will need a simple trick to memorize them more easily.

Before making mental images of the words for which you do not have a meaning, you should first create *a sound-alike substitute* for the word. This is a familiar word that sounds similar to the difficult word you want to remember.

For example, you can remember the word "*pollination*" (a biology scientific term meaning "*transfer of the fine spores that contain male gametes"),* by using the sound-alike: "*Polynesian.*"

If some of your associations produce words that don't quite match the correct pronunciation of your word, don't worry. Concentrate on the phonetic sound of a new word, rather than how it is led spelled. Just focus on the triggers that will remind you of the difficult word and leave the pronunciation details for later. Also, your sound-alike mnemonic doesn't need to include all the sounds of the word you want to memorize. Usually, it's enough to remember the beginning of words, and your brain will fill in the rest.

For longer words, you may have to split them into two or more convenient parts, create sound-likes to each part and then associate them with individual images.

To show you how The Sound-Alike Technique works, let's view some examples:

1. How To Remember Definitions of Unfamiliar Words

The word "*Belonephobia*" means an irrational fear of needles and pins, usually resulting in abnormal behavior and anxiety. The word comes from the Greek words: "belon" (meaning "*needle*") and phobia (meaning "*fear*").

For the word "belon", we can easily find a sound-alike substitute in English: "balloon", while the word "phobia" is synonymous with the word "fear".

The fear of needles (Belonephobia) can be remembered by the sentence *"The balloon is afraid of needles"*

2. How to Learn New Words from a Foreign Language

Learning the vocabulary of a foreign language can be fun if you apply your ability for creative word associations.

If a new word resembles a word in your native language, create a mental image association between the native word and the new word.

For example, the french word "*tromper*" means to cheat. You can associate it with the English word "*trumpet*" and *a liar* (Pinocchio). Similar, the word meaning "*father*" in French, is "*pere*". Associate father to pear and you'll always remember it. The Spanish word "*hermano*" means "brother." You can imagine your brother as "an air-man."

In this way, you can learn any new word, by using your current existing knowledge as foundations.

3. How to Remember People's Names using the Sound-Alike Method

Memorizing names is a general problem of our memory because names are abstract concepts and difficult to visualize for our brains. The solution is to transform the name, ever since you first heard it, into a concrete and memorable image. If you meet a person whose name has no meaning for you, The Sound-Alike Method is perfect to memorize its name, by breaking it down into a substitute word or idea. For example, if you meet Mr. Baldwin, you might think of a *"bald twin*". In the same way, Bill could become "*a dollar bill*" and Jane might become "*a chain*". Just use the associations that come into your brain naturally, these are the ones your memory will find easiest to recall.

How to recognize where to use this technique with the SCALM Method?

Whenever we have to learn difficult words in your native language or a foreign language, people's names, botanical, geographical, or other scientific names, The Sound-Alike Method is the most effective memory technique to use.

Memory Technique #4: Rhymes and Jingles

Two other simple techniques that can help you turn abstract information into memorable things are rhymes and jingles. Music, and especially the lyrics put on music, is still an extremely efficient vehicle to forming new memories, especially for predominantly auditory persons.

Like song lyrics, rhymes and jingles are so easily recalled that they stick in our brain, which is very receptive to auditory stimuli. Just think about how easy you can instantly recognize a known tune only by hearing a few musical notes. You may not recall the name of the song but you do know that you have heard it before.

Let' view how these techniques work to help you memorize different concepts:

1. **Rhymes** are short verses used to remember data.

Even though they are not usually accompanied by music, their rhythmic sonority makes them extremely easy to memorize by the brain.

You can use rhymes to help you remember things, people, places, or lists of concepts. You have probably learned a number of these in school to help you remember new concepts and historical references.

Here is an example:

"30 Days has September
April, June, and November
All the rest have 31
Except for February alone
Which has but 28 days clear?
And 29 in each leap year"

And here is another example of a rhyme used for remembering Roman Numerals:

***"I** am a Roman soldier 1*

*5 **V**ictories I have won*

***X** marks the spot where 10 comrades fell*

*Only 50 **L**ived to tell*

*100 more were **captured** in war*

*Now we fight 500 **D**ays more*

*1000 soldiers **M**arching on tour"*

With practice, you can develop your talent for writing rhymes. The basic rule is to keep your rhymes short and simple.

Define the key information you want to remember and chunk it down into a series of short phrases or concepts. Then look at the last words in the sentences: can you rhyme any of them? If they don't rhyme, can you replace or add a word to create the rhyme?

2. **Jingles** are phrases set to music, so that the music helps trigger your memory.

Because songs are easier to remember than just words, jingles are commonly used by advertisers to make an ad more memorable.

There are two approaches by which you can use jingles as memory techniques. The first is to start with a familiar tune and to create alternate lyrics, by replacing original words with the items you want to memorize. The second approach is to try reading your learning material aloud, in a hip-hop music style.

Think about what rhymes and jingles you have used in the past, and, if you feel creatively inspired, create your auditory mnemonics to help you remember your material.

With a little creativity, these two simple techniques can be applied to memorize single words or lists of words, general information, formulas, and even complex concepts.

Memory Technique #5: How to Remember People's Names

Another important difficulty in the learning process is the memorization of the names of people we find in the texts to be learned. This is a general problem of our memory, which is because names are abstract and difficult to visualize concepts for the brain, as opposed to human faces, which are essentially images, therefore much easier to remember. If you will be able to associate a concrete image to the name from the beginning, it will be difficult not to remember it later.

The good news is that there is several number scientifically proven ways to remember people's names. Although on the internet you can find numerous tips on how to remember the people's names, in this lesson I will present you with a very simple method that can help you develop this skill, known as *"The Names Association Technique"*.

Here are the steps this technique:

Step 1. Pay Attention

The first step is to pay attention when you read someone's name. If you don't catch the person's name the first time, pause your lecture and repeat it to yourself mentally. That way, you will transfer the name from your working to your long-term memory.

If you have a picture of the person in your material, carefully observe his face and think if the name matches his figure.

Step 2. Create an image from a person's name

When you first read or hear a person's name, immediately create an image in association with it. A name doesn't mean anything to your brain; for this reason, a mental picture of it is not easily formed. To memorize names to go with faces, names need to be translated into images.

The secret to memorizing names is to attach significance to them, by translating them into concrete and easy to remember images of known people, objects, or animals.

There are three ways to create this visual association:

a) If the name already has a meaning, such as Carpenter or Wolf, use that, like imagining Martin Wolf as a wolf dressed as a grandmother.

b) If the name doesn't immediately have a meaning, as is true of most names, see if you can come up with other memorable associations. For example, if the person's name is Jackson, you might think of Michael Jackson; if the person's name is Jordan, you might think of the basketball player Michael Jordan.

c) If the name has no meaning, you can break down the word into a substitute word or idea, using the Sound-Alike Method. For example, if you meet Mr. Lawrence, you might think of some *"lower ants"* , if you meet a "Paul," you might think of a *"ball,"* and if you meet a "Mike" you might think of *"a microphone"*. Think of something that sounds enough like the name to remind you of it. Just think of whatever first comes to mind and use the associations that come into your brain naturally-these are the ones your memory will find easiest to recall.

The material you have to learn may contain the material you have to learn may contain a lot of names. In this situation, you will have to repeatedly apply the technique of associating names with memorable images, so you might think to create a **pre-defined list of associations** for the most common names.

Here are some examples from the two times USA Memory Champion Ron White:

"Anthony = ants in a tree,

Abby= a bee,

Jim= gym,

Beth = bath,

Claudia= cloud,

Carmen= car and man, etc"

So, whenever you have to memorize the names of people, you can apply this simple method to associate them with a concrete and easy to memorize image.

Memory Technique #6: Memorize Numbers with the Major System

Probably the most abstract and difficult to remember things for our brains are numbers.

But why is it so difficult to remember a sequence of numbers, even after seeing it just a few moments before? Contrary to concrete concepts, that can be associated with an object, numbers are difficult to remember because they are abstract concepts. If I say: *"think of an orange"*, your mind immediately visualizes an orange. But if I say 465257653, you will have a hard time committing it to memory.

To be an effective learner, you must be able to remember a lot of numbers, or you'll end up getting all confused. In almost everything we have to learn, there are numbers involved: dates, calculations, statistics, percent, and many others. Whether you love them or you hate them, numbers will not go away.

For this reason, memory experts have invented many efficient methods for memorizing numbers. Of these, I chose to use within the SCALM method a very simple, but extremely efficient technique, known as "*The Major System.*"

The Major System is a very efficient technique used to memorize numbers, shuffled playing cards, dates, historical facts, and other abstract sequences of items.

Created in the mid 17th century, it has been used and continually improved upon for more than 300 years and now is one of the most used memory techniques in memory competitions. One of the reasons is that it is easier to learn than other memory systems and also it is fun to use.

About this technique, teach expert Tony Buzan, co-founder of world Memory Championships, wrote:

"The Major System is the Ultimate Memory System."

The Major system is based on the principle that images can be remembered more easily than numbers. By using images, large amounts of information can be accurately memorized.

It works by converting number sequences into consonants, consonants into images, and linking images into little stories. Thus, by transforming the numbers into memorable images, we create unforgettable memories for them.

Let's see how the Major Memory System works in practice:

First of all, you need to pre-learn a simple 10 associations code that links the digits from 0 to 9 and the following consonant sounds:

- 0(Zero) is S, Z or soft-C
- 1 is D, T or Th
- 2 is N
- 3 is M
- 4 is R
- 5 is L
- 6 is J, Sh, soft-Ch, Dg or soft-G

- 7 is K, hard-Ch, hard-C, hard-G or Ng
- 8 is F or V
- 9 is P or B

This code is an essential tool of the Major System, so to effectively encode numbers, by transforming them into memorable images, but also to decode these images later, you need to know it very well. It is easy to learn (it shouldn't take more than 30 minutes to fully master it) and, once learned, it can be used for life.

The reason why this technique uses consonants is that, usually, in a word, consonants are the ones that define the meaning and the way it sounds. The vowels are just the filling between its consonants. If you hear the word “Rat”, it is defined primarily by the 2 consonants: R and T.

The Major System helps you turn abstract numbers into consonants and then into memorable words.

After you have learned this simple code, the next step of the Major System is to apply the code to transform the numbers into simple and concrete images.

You take a number you would like to remember and apply *the CODE*, by creating mental associations between numbers to be remembered and the consonants from the previous list.

These consonants grouped in twos will create a structure around which you will create a word, by filling the gaps with "neutral" elements (vowel sounds). For example, the number 32(MN), can become the word "*MaN*".

The number sequences are converted into consonants from the learned code, then into words. The words are formed quite simply, by filling in the gaps between consonants with vowels.

This 4 digits number: 9534 can be translated into 4 consonants: P-L-M-R, which can become the word 'PaLMeR'.

Please note that this is not the best example. In order to be effective, **it is recommended to use the Major system to numbers of maximum 2 digits**, so if the sequence you have to memorize has more digits, you will have to chunk it into groups of 2s, then to create more simple words (for example, PLMR, spitted in PL and MR, can become "Play More")

As another example, let's take the number 1402.

According to the system's code, the digits in the number 1402 translate to *D, R, S, N.* Now, we need to form one or more words with these letters.

These letters can become the words: "*Dear Sean*", or "*Door Sauna*".

As you can see, both variants can become memorable images.

Remember that conversions are based on how the words sound, not how they're spelled. This is why the Majors System is also known as "*the phonetic mnemonic System.*"

When you recall your word associated with the number, you would know that it could represent only that number because the consonant letter in the word represents no other number, and vowels do not count as numbers in the Major system.

When you choose your words, I recommend you to create your images, based on the associations that come to your mind with ease, according to your way of thinking. At first, the conversion process may seem a bit slow and complicated, but with just a little bit of practice, it becomes second nature.

Once you've turned your number into words, you can create a little story to memorize them in order.

Here is an example:

The Major System is a very efficient technique for memorizing dates.

"Let's say that you have an appointment with Bill on September 3 at 7.15 PM, and you need to memorize this date.

The first step is to transform the date and hour into numbers: 09-03-19-15.

Then, apply the major system's code: SP-SM-DB-TL.

The 4 numbers can become the words: SouP-SwiM-DuBai- hoTeL.

Now, let's create a little story with these words: "Imagine your friend Bill swimming in a soup bowl in a Dubai Hotel." With this image, you will not be able to forget about your appointment with your friend."

You can memorize the birthdays of your friends by using the same method. In this case, there is no need to memorize the year, but only the month and the day.

Let's say that you have a friend whose birthday is on July 20. The first step is to transform the data into numbers: ***07-20.*** *By using the Major System,* ***07-20*** *becomes-**SK-NS. SK** might become the word "Sock", while **NS** might become the word "Nose"*

Imagine your friend with smelly sock blocking his nose, and you will never forget his birthday!

The Applications of the Major System

As a result of its intrinsic logic, this technique is very easy to learn and you can begin using it immediately. You can apply it to the memorization of numbers, dates in history, birthdays and anniversaries, lists and information for examinations.

This technique passed to a higher level by developing a more complex code, is also used by mental athletes in memory competitions, to memorize numbers or playing cards. For this purpose, to become more efficient, they create their own (more complex) codes, which they pre-learn to help them from their mental images quickly. Thus, for numbers memorization, most of them have a personalized code for the first 100 numbers (by assigning a distinctive word to each number from zero to 99), and a code of 52 images for playing cards(one for each card).

But, for the SCALM method, the basic level of the major system presented in this lesson is sufficient.

Now you know that, when you have to memorize numbers and data, the Major System is the technique you can use for this purpose.

How to Choose the Techniques

The SCALM method is a very effective learning tool because it combines these powerful memory techniques. Scientists agree that learning is about recognizing and memorizing patterns.

But how to recognize what technique should we use when memorizing different types of information?

After in previous lessons we saw that each memory technique has certain applicability, now let's see what are **the SCALM rules of association by type of materials to be learned:**

1. Lists of concepts

The most common type of process information that you will have to remember will be in the form of a list of concepts. As I said earlier, almost everything we have to learn can easily turn into a list, by splitting the concepts up into small pieces or "chunks" of information. Therefore, the result of the chunking process will most often be a list of items that you will have to memorize by applying one of the specific methods:

- **Acronyms**- can be used for small lists (of up to 7-8 items);
- **The Sentence Method** is better for longer lists as compared to the Acronym Method, because a sentence allows you to create much more elaborate mnemonic images than a single word. But this is also limited to the length of a sentence that is easily memorable, meaning lists of maximum 15-20 items;
- For longer lists, an appropriate method is **the Story Technique**, because a story can be much longer, but at the same time it remains extremely memorable;
- If you are an auditory learner, especially if you have a penchant for poetry, it will be easy for you to use **Rhymes** and **Jingles** to create mnemonics for your lists.

2. Numbers and dates

Another type of information that you will have to remember will be **numbers and dates**. For these, I presented earlier a very efficient method called The Major System.

Here is how it works:

Let's say you have to memorize this historical event: "*In 1961 Yuri Gagarin of USSR becomes the first spaceman.*"

First, memorize the year with the Major System. The 4 digits of the year 1961 are converted into sounds, then into images: *1961 becomes TB and JT, which can be "Tube" and "Jet".*

The action of the date (the event) becomes the third image "Yuri Gagarin flying around the Earth"

Now, we have 3 images that only need to be linked in a memorable scene: *"You can imagine a cosmonaut riding a jet tube around the Earth"*

Let's see some other examples:

• *"In 1453 Turks captured Constantinople."* With the Major System, 1453 becomes TR and LM, which can be: "Tour" and "Helm". You can imagine a Turk soldier making a tour of Constantinople with a motorcycle helmet on his head.

• *"In 1895 Roentgen discovered X-Rays."* 18-95 becomes "TV" and "Pool". Imagine Rontgen throwing a TV in the pool and X-rays coming out of it.

3. Difficult words

Another type of hard-to-remember information you will encounter in your learning process is the difficult terms, regardless of whether they are difficult words in your native language or foreign, words that you aren't familiar with.

The most effective way to learn these words is "*The Sound-Alike Method*".

Before making mental images of the words to which you do not have a meaning, you should first create a sound-alike substitute for the word. This is a familiar word that sounds similar to the difficult word you want to remember.

For example, to memorize the Latin name of cabbage (*"Brassica oleracea"),* you can use the sound-alike: "*Brass Car All over Asia*", then link this image with the plant.

4. People's Names

To memorize people's names, you need to attach significance to them, by translating them into concrete and easy to remember images of known people, objects, or animals. I have already shown you a method by which you can associate any name with either a known person who has that name or with a pre-defined list of associations for the most common names.

You can also use the Sound Alike technique to transform the name into an easy to remember the image. For example, the name Julie might prompt an image of "*jewelry*" because the words sound similar, while Bill might make you think of "*a dollar bill*".

These are the general rules for choosing the memory techniques to use in your associations. However, I recommend that you stay creative and flexible in choosing and using them. There are no rigid rules for choosing the right method; you just have to follow your instinct. As you gain experience in using the method, you will immediately recognize what memory technique you can apply to that chunk.

Then, I recommend you consider combining two or more methods for memorizing more complex chunks of information. Thus, to memorize a larger paragraph, you can, for example, combine **The Story Method** with **The Sound-Alike Method** , to create a more memorable image.

If you have to remember mixed information, like the atomic numbers and the name of the chemical elements, you can combine **the Major System** with **the Sound Alike Method** to get a memorable image.

Here are some examples:

The chemical element *Krypton* has atomic number 36.For Krypton, we can use the sound-alike “Kryptonite”, while 36, in the Major System, is M-Ch, or Mach. *“Imagine Superman flying at Mach speed and searching for kryptonite”*

The chemical element *Titanium* has atomic number 22.For Titanium, we can use the sound-alike “Titanic” and 22, in the Major System, is NN, or Nixon. *“Imagine the Ship Titanic sinking, with Nixon on the deck”.*

Now that I have finished presenting the memory techniques, we have reached the point where we can continue our previous example. It took this long presentation of memory techniques, for you to understand better how they work.

Here we were with our example, at the end of step 2 of the SCALM method. We have this list of items, which we have to transform into easy-to-remember images, applying the methods you just learned:

1.Rising
Risings of the peasantry took place in various parts of Germany, notably in Swabia, Thuringia, the Rhine Provinces, and Saxony (1524).
Thomas Munzer, the leader of the Anabaptists, encouraged them in their fight for freedom.
At first the attack was directed principally against the spiritual princes. Many monasteries and churches were plundered, and several of the nobles were put to death.
Soon the lay princes of Germany, alarmed by the course of the revolutionaries and fearing for the safety of their own territories, assembled their forces and marched against the insurgents.
2.The War
The war was carried on mercilessly on both sides, close upon 100,000 peasants being killed in the field, while many of their leaders, amongst them Thomas Munzer, were arrested and condemned to death.
In nearly every important engagement the peasants, as might be expected, suffered defeat, so that before the end of 1525 the movement was, practically speaking, at an end.
3.Luther's reaction
Luther, who had been consulted by both sides, and who had tried to avoid committing himself to either, frightened by the very violence of the storm he had been instrumental in creating, issued an appeal to the princes calling upon them to show no mercy to the forces of disorder,
4.Melanchthon's reaction
And even Melanchthon, gentle and moderate as he usually was, did not hesitate to declare that the peasants of Germany had more liberty than should be allowed to such rude and uncultured people.
5.Conclusions of the war

The Peasants' War, disastrous as it was, did some good by opening men's eyes to the dangerous consequences of Luther's extravagant harangues,
And by giving some slight indications as to the real character and methods of the man, who was posing as a heaven-sent reformer and at the same time as a champion of popular liberty.

Now the magic will happen. Let's see how it's done:

The first chunk is about the year of rising and about a few German states where the uprising started.

1.Rising
Risings of the peasantry took place in various parts of Germany, notably in Swabia, Thuringia, the Rhine Provinces, and Saxony (1524).

As you already know now, the memory technique used for dates and numbers is the Major System. The year 1524 is transformed into two groups of consonants: TL and NR, which can become the words ***Towel*** and ***Nero***. If you have other preferences, I have nothing against choosing other words, but these came to my mind first. Therefore, the first image I will note in my list will be that of the *"**Emperor Nero burning a towel.**"**(1)***

Then, we have this list of German states: Swabia, Thuringia, Rhine Provinces, Saxony.

You've probably noticed that for this small list we should apply the acronym method, but being too many consonants, it's hard to create a memorable acronym for this list, so I will apply The Sentence Method and I will get this image to add to my list: ***"Sad Tiger Releases Snakes"(2).***

The next chunk is about Thomas Munzer, who encouraged the peasants to fight for freedom:

Thomas Munzer, the leader of the Anabaptists, encouraged them in their fight for freedom.

First of all, in this text we have to remember a not too common name, for which we will have to apply one of the learned memory techniques. By applying The Sound-Alike Method, I can transform the name Munzer into the words: ***"Moon"*** and ***"Sir"***, which I could associate with the image of ***"Sir Tom Jones singing at the moon and pointing to the Statue of Liberty."(3)***

The next chunk is about plundered churches, and nobles put to death.

At first the attack was directed principally against the spiritual princes. Many monasteries and churches were plundered, and several of the nobles were put to death.

In this case, it is very simple to associate memorable images. I will note on my list" **across"(4)**, representing the churches, and "**a sword"(5)** representing the killed nobles.

Then, we have this chunk about mobilizing the army, for which I will note on my list the image of **"a bugle calling for the attack".(6)**

Soon, the lay princes of Germany, alarmed by the course of the revolutionaries and fearing for the safety of their own territories, assembled their forces and marched against the insurgents.

The paragraph about the war has three main ideas: the 100k victims, the arrest and death sentence of Thomas Munzer, and the year the war ended - 1525.

2.The War
The war was carried on mercilessly on both sides, close upon 100,000 peasants being killed in the field, while many of their leaders, amongst them Thomas Munzer, were arrested and condemned to death.
In nearly every important engagement the peasants, as might be expected, suffered defeat, so that before the end of 1525 the movement was, practically speaking, at an end.

I will note on my list these 3 images:

- **"100k dead bodies"(7)**,
- "**Tom Jones with handcuffs and executed**, and,
- for the year 1525, by applying the Major System, I get the words Tall and Neil, so I will use the image of **a very tall Neil Armstrong. (8)**

Then, we have a paragraph about Luther being consulted by both parties and about his call for ruthless intervention against rebels.

3.Luther's reaction
Luther, who had been consulted by both sides, and who had tried to avoid committing himself to either, frightened by the very violence of the storm he had been instrumental in creating, issued an appeal to the princes calling upon them to show no mercy to the forces of disorder

For this, I will use the image of **"Martin Luther King wearing two stethoscopes, and calling 911 from his phone."(9)**

The next paragraph contains another very difficult name to remember (Melanchthon), so I'll use the Sound-Alike Method again to turn it into an easy to memorize image: **"melancholy tone, being heard from a large Liberty bell."(10)**

4.Melanchthon's reaction
and even Melanchthon, gentle and moderate as he usually was, did not hesitate to declare that the peasants of Germany had more liberty than should be allowed to such rude and uncultured people.

The final paragraph is about *"opening men's eyes to the dangerous consequences of Luther's extravagant harangues"* and about the character of this man" *who was posing as a heaven-sent reformer and at the same time as a champion of popular liberty."*

5.Conclusions of the war
The Peasants' War, disastrous as it was, did some good by opening men's eyes to the dangerous consequences of Luther's extravagant harangues,
and by giving some slight indications as to the real character and methods of the man, who was posing as a heaven-sent reformer and at the same time as a champion of popular liberty.

For this chunk, I will create the image of "**Martin Luther King wearing a large pair of extravagant glasses, posing in heaven near the Statue of Liberty"(11).**

At the end of this association step, we have a series of simple and easy to memorize images, which we will place in order along with a structure that will help us to memorize them in order. This structure is created by using the Memory Palace Technique, which I will present to you in the next chapter.

Chapter Nine: Step 4. Locate

After you learned, in previous chapters, how to transform abstract information into concrete images, now you will need a mental structure where to place your mental images, to help you memorize them in order. For this purpose, the SCALM method uses a very efficient technique known as the Memory Palace (or LOCI) Technique.

This ancient method is literally the king of memory techniques. Its power is so incredible, that all memory athletes use it invariably, in their memory training and in memory competitions.

The scientists have discovered that, when the memory athletes memorize information, they use a region in their brains, the hippocampus, that is especially important for spatial memory and navigation. It is the same way that a taxi driver uses his brain to navigate within a large city.

But why would the brain of a mental athlete look like the brain of a taxi driver? Because memory training is very much like a mental journey along some imaginary routes, having certain images placed in pre-defined places.

So, in short, the memory palace method works like this: You take with you the images you want to memorize and then embark on an imaginary journey through a place you know well, such as your home or your daily commute to work. Then, in different places that follow a certain order, you place a picture and make a mental connection between it and that place.

For example, you could imagine *"an elephant eating in your living room"*, then *"a crocodile in your bathtub"* and then *"Angelina Jolie washing dishes in your kitchen"*. All of these images, personalized by your mind, are extremely powerful triggers for your memories. When you want to remember these items again, you simply go through the route markers in the same sequence and all the images will appear in your mind's eye.

The memory palace technique is based on the fact that it is easier to remember new information that is linked to the information you already have, which in this case, is your memory palace. In this way, the technique uses familiar locations to help you memorize important information.

The most common type of memory palace involves making a mental journey through a familiar place like your home or your town. Along that journey, there are specific locations that you always visit in the same order, so you can create a path in your mind's eye, made up of places that you know well, and can easily visualize, then populate this places with images representing whatever you want to remember.

Each stage of those routes can be used as a mental peg, where to hang on some images that help you form the associations needed for memorization.

Memory palaces don't necessarily have to be buildings. They can be routes through your neighborhood, or they can be routes in your favorite computer game.

They can be real or imaginary, indoors or outdoors, so long as there's some order that links one place to the next, and so long as they are very familiar to you. It is recommended to prepare your memory palaces beforehand, and even to develop your own collection of memory palaces to rotate their use for different materials, because they can be reused after some time.

Now, let's apply the memory palace technique to memorize the list of images from our example started earlier:

In this example, I will use a hypothetical mental journey, but assuming that you will use a memory palace that you know very well, such as your home, the images will become much more memorable for you.

In the first place of my memory palace, my front door, I will place the first image from my list, which is that of "*Emperor Nero burning a towel next to a sad tiger releasing snakes*" **(1)**. By adding, in my mind, as many details about this scene that is happening right there, it will be easily recorded in my memory. By the way, the expressions: "*in the first place*", "*in the second place*" and the like, originated in this ancient technique that associates memories with various physical places.

Then, in my living room, I can imagine "*Sir Tom Jones singing under the moon and pointing to the Statue of Liberty*" **(2).**

In my kitchen, I imagine "*across with a sword*"**(3)** and *"a soldier with a bugle, calling for the attack"***(4)**.

On my stairs, I imagine "*Tom Jones in handcuffs being executed by a very tall Neil Armstrong"***(5).**

In my bathroom," *Martin Luther King wearing two stethoscopes, calling 911 from his phone" **(6).***

In the next room, a can see *"a large Liberty bell sounding a melancholy tone"* **(7).**

And in my dressing, which is the final place of my journey, I will put the image of "*Martin Luther King wearing a large pair of extravagant glasses, posing in heaven near the Statue of Liberty*"**(8)**.

So, we have some memorable images, which we placed along a structure that will help us to memorize them in order, and we almost memorized them. That tangled historical text has been transformed into easy-to-remember images.

Now we have reached the end of the work of reorganizing our mental images. All we have to do now is to memorize the images created so far, and we will do it in the next chapter.

Chapter Ten: Step 5. Memorize

The final step of the SCALM technique is memorization, when you rehearse the learned material in your mind, by walking again mentally along your memory palace and remembering the items you placed there, in order from start to finish.

At this stage, we do not have much to do, except to complete our mental journey again and to visualize the mental images.

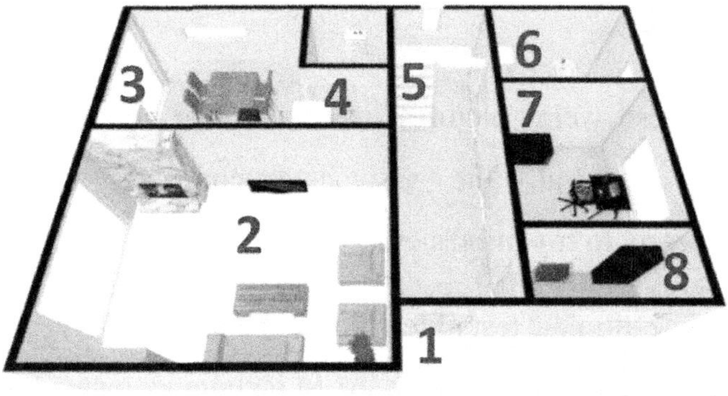

In the first place of my memory palace, my front door, I can see "*Emperor Nero burning a towel next to a sad tiger releasing snakes*" **(1)**. Then, in my living room,

I can imagine "*Sir Tom Jones singing under the moon and pointing to the Statue of Liberty*" **(2).** In my kitchen, I see "*across with a sword*"**(3)** and "*a soldier with a bugle, calling for the attack*"**(4)**. On my stairs, I see "*Tom Jones in handcuffs being executed by a very tall Neil Armstrong*"**(5),** while in my bathroom I can see "*Martin Luther King wearing two stethoscopes, calling 911 from his phone*" ***(6).*** In the next room, a can see "*a large Liberty bell sounding a melancholy tone*"**(7)**, and in my dressing, I can see "*Martin Luther King wearing a large pair of extravagant glasses, posing in heaven near the Statue of Liberty* "**(8)**.

These weird pictures just stuck like glue in my memory and all the associated concepts appear immediately in my mind's eye.

The ultimate test of learning is the process of recall. By using the 5 steps of the SCALM technique, instead of making random memorization, you learned in a proactive and organized way, and you will be able to recall the firmly memorized information.

You've just learned to use the most powerful existing learning technique! This method will help you learn any material, whether it is a speech you have to present in front of an audience, or a book you have to learn for your studies.Even though the example I presented to you so far was a rather short text, the SCALM method is very efficient even when memorizing entire books. The steps are the same; the only difference is the length of mental journeys you will need to use.

The next part is dedicated to practical activities. You will see some more complex examples, which I am sure will convince you that the SCALM method is a universal technique, applicable to any type of information that you may have to learn, regardless of whether it is biology, chemistry, history, medicine, the vocabulary of a foreign language, physics, mathematics or coding.

All you have to do is follow the 5 steps of the method to create memorable associations, then place them along a mental journey. See you in the next chapter!

PART IV: The Practical Part of this Book

Chapter Eleven: Practical Example #1. Memorize a Speech

A. The Learning Material (A Speech)

"Tips for Improving Your Memory"

By Chris M Nemo

"A good memory is essential for a student, executive, employee, politician – in fact for everyone in every walk of life. It is necessary, too, in social life; for a person who forgets his social engagements and never remembers the faces of those he met, it will never be a social success. Memory plays a big role in our life.

Today, I will present you with the most effective tips from the memory experts, to help you to improve your memory.

1. Cultivate your memory

Use your memory and place confidence in it. One of the important things in the cultivation of memory is the actual use of it. Do not allow your memory to atrophy.

2. Review and Rehearse

In review, you go over what you have just learned to more firmly encode it in the first place;

in rehearsal, you expand on your initial review with a return to the material, so you firmly fix that encoding in place.

3. Involve all your senses

You can strengthen your memory by involving various senses and recalling the information to relate the data. An impression received through more senses is stronger as one received through but one of these channels.

4. Strong first impression

Get into the habit of fixing a clear and strong impression from the first. Your first impression must be strong and firm enough to serve as a basis for subsequent ones. Otherwise, each time you revive an impression, it will not include details omitted in the first one.

5. Persist until you learn the Memory Improvement Techniques

Techniques can be somewhat complicated – until you learn them, that is. Like driving or using a computer, once you learn the "whys and how's," you never really need to think much about them after that. Once the memory techniques are imprinted in your brain, they become a natural process

6. You are a part of the story!

You will remember more information if you try to relate that information to yourself. By putting yourself in the story created from mnemonic images, you somehow trick your brain into believing that the experience has happened to you

Now you know that to improve your memory you need a few "crispy" things:
CULTIVATE YOUR MEMORY, REVIEW AND REHEARSE, INVOLVE ALL YOUR SENSES, A STRONG FIRST IMPRESSION, PERSISTENCE IN LEARNING THE MEMORY IMPROVEMENT TECHNIQUES, AND TO PUT YOURSELF IN THE STORY

The journey of memory improvement does not end. But it does get more interesting because you will begin to memorize easily anything you want.

None of the top memory experts would claim to be born with a great memory. All of them have learned all the necessary techniques to develop their skills, and have practiced to a high level to get them to the top of this skill.

You can do the same!

Why not start today?

You too can become a mental athlete!"

B. Apply The SCALM Technique

1. Structure of the information

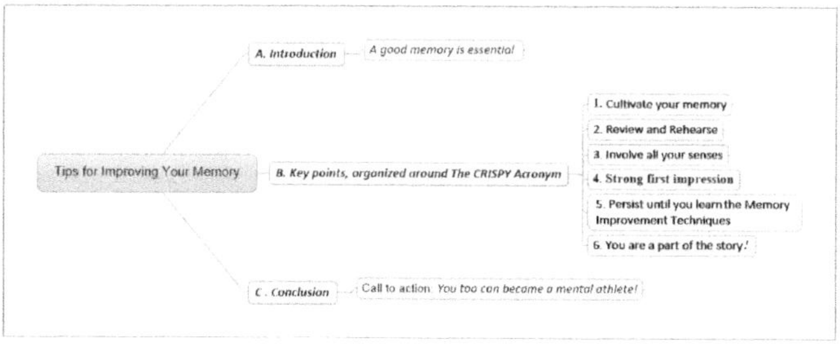
Tips for Improving Your Memory
A. Introduction
A good memory is essential
B. Key points, organized around The CRISPY Acronym
1. Cultivate your memory
2. Review and Rehearse
3. Involve all your senses
4. Strong first impression
5. Persist until you learn the Memory Improvement Techniques
6. You are a part of the story!
C. Conclusion
Call to action: You too can become a mental athlete!

2. Chunk the material

The Chunks:
A good memory is essential for every student, politician, executive, or employee– in fact for everyone in every walk of life. *It is necessary, too, in social life; for a person who forgets his social engagements and never remembers the faces of those he met, it will never be a social success.* *Memory plays a big role in our life.*

Today, I will present you with the most effective tips from the memory experts, to help you to improve your memory. ***Cultivate your memory*** ***Review and Rehearse*** ***Involve all your senses*** ***Strong first impression*** ***Persist until you learn the memory techniques*** ***You are a part of the story!***
1. Cultivate your memory *Use your memory and place confidence in it. One of the important things in the cultivation of memory is the actual use of it. Do not allow your memory to atrophy.*
2. Review and Rehearse *In review, you go over what you have just learned to more firmly encode it in the first place;* *in rehearsal, you expand on your initial review with a return to the material, so you firmly fix that encoding in place.*
3. Involve all your senses *You can strengthen your memory by involving various senses and recalling the information to relate the data. An impression received through more senses is stronger as one received through but one of these channels.*
4.Strong first impression *Get into the habit of fixing a clear and strong impression from the first. Your first impression must be strong and firm enough to serve as a basis for subsequent ones. Otherwise, each time you revive an impression, it will not include details omitted in the first one.*

5.Persist until you learn the memory improvement techniques *Techniques can be somewhat complicated – until you learn them, that is. Like driving or using a computer, once you learn the "whys and haws," you never really need to think much about them after that. Once the memory techniques are imprinted in your brain, they become a natural process.*
6. You are a part of the story! *You will remember more information if you try to relate that information to yourself. By putting yourself in the story created from mnemonic images, you somehow trick your brain into believing that the experience has happened to you.*

The journey of memory improvement does not end. But it does get more interesting because you will begin to memorize easily anything you want.

None of the top memory experts would claim to be born with a great memory. All of them have learned all the necessary techniques to develop their skills, and have practiced to a high level to get them to the top of this skill.

You can do the same!

Why not start today?

You too can become a mental athlete!

3. Associate the chunks with simple images

The Chunks	The Associations	The Images
A good memory is essential for every student, politician, executive, or employee– in fact for everyone in every walk of life. *It is necessary, too, in social life; for a person who forgets his social engagements and never remembers the faces of those he met, it will never be a social success.* *Memory plays a big role in our life.*	Essence Social network An actress	 
Today, I will present you with the most effective tips from the memory experts, to help you to improve your memory. ***Cultivate your memory*** ***Review and Rehearse*** ***Involve all your senses*** ***Strong first impression***	*A Bag of Crispy Minis*	

Persist until you learn the memory techniques ***You are a part of the story!*** *(The CRISPY acronym)*		
1. Cultivate your memory *Use your memory and place confidence in it. One of the important things in the cultivation of memory is the actual use of it. Do not allow your memory to atrophy.*	Handshake A Training Dumbbell	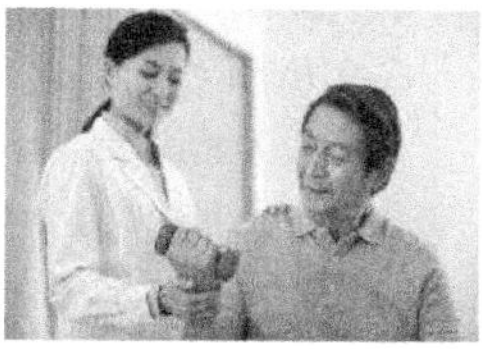
2. Review and Rehearse *In review, you go over what you have just learned to more firmly encode it in the first place;* *in rehearsal, you expand on your initial review with a return to the material, so you firmly fix that encoding in place.*	A Pair of Glasses A Movie Screen	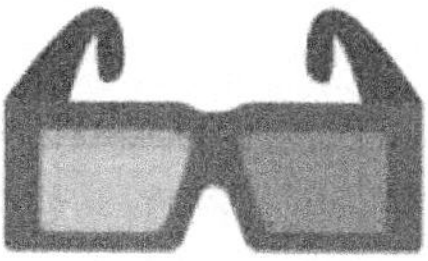 
3. Involve all your senses *You can strengthen your memory by involving various senses and recalling the information*	Pick a flower and smell it	

to relate the data. An impression received through more senses is stronger as one received through but one of these channels.		
4.Strong first impression *Get into the habit of fixing a clear and strong impression from the first. Your first impression must be strong and firm enough to serve as a basis for subsequent ones. Otherwise, each time you revive an impression, it will not include details omitted in the first one.*	A *Photo Camera*	
5.Persist until you learn the memory improvement techniques *Techniques can be somewhat complicated – until you learn them, that is. Like driving or using a computer, once you learn the "whys and how's," you never really need to think much about them*	A teacher (Find a particular teacher from your past or present. It is important	

after that. Once the memory techniques are imprinted in your brain, they become a natural process.	to be a known person to you)	
6. You are a part of the story!*You will remember more information if you try to relate that information to yourself. By putting yourself in the story created from mnemonic images, you somehow trick your brain into believing that the experience has happened to you*	*A Fairy Tale Book*	

The journey of memory improvement does not end. But it does get more interesting because you will begin to memorize easily anything you want.	A Suitcase	
None of the top memory experts would claim to be born with a great memory. All of them have learned all the necessary techniques to develop their skills, and have practiced to a high level to get them to the top of this skill.	A Memory Expert (e.g. Dominic O'Brien) training his memory	
You can do the same! Why not start today? You too can become a mental athlete!	A Gold Medal	

4. Locate (Put the images in a memory palace)

TIP: It's always o good option to create a journey in logical order across the same room where you are supposed to give a speech. By memorizing the points of your speech in this way, you will have visual reminders everywhere around you, in the room, and they will automatically trigger the key ideas of your speech.

5. Memorize the images...and you will know your Speech

A good memory is essential(1) ...It is necessary, too, in social life(2) ...Memory plays a big role(3) in our life...

*The most effective tips from the memory experts, to help you to improve your memory-**CRISPY acronym** (4)*

Cultivate your memory *Use your memory and place confidence(5) in it. One of the important things in the cultivation of memory is the actual use of it(6). Do not allow your memory to atrophy...*

Review and Rehearse *In review(7), you go over what you have just learned to more firmly encode it in the first place; in rehearsal(8), you expand on your initial review with a return to the material, so you firmly fix that encoding in place.*

Involve all your senses *You can strengthen your memory by involving various senses(9)...*

Strong first impression *Get into the habit of fixing a clear and strong impression (10) from the first...*

Persist until you learn the memory improvement techniques: *Techniques can be somewhat complicated – until you learn them(11), that is...*

You are a part of the story! (12) *You will remember more information if you try to relate that information to yourself. ...*

The journey(13) of memory improvement does not end. ....None of the top memory experts(14) would claim to be born with a great memory. ...You too can become a mental athlete! (15).

Chapter Twelve: Practical Example #2. Memorize The Periodic Table of Chemical Elements

A. The Learning Material (Periodic Table of Chemical Elements)

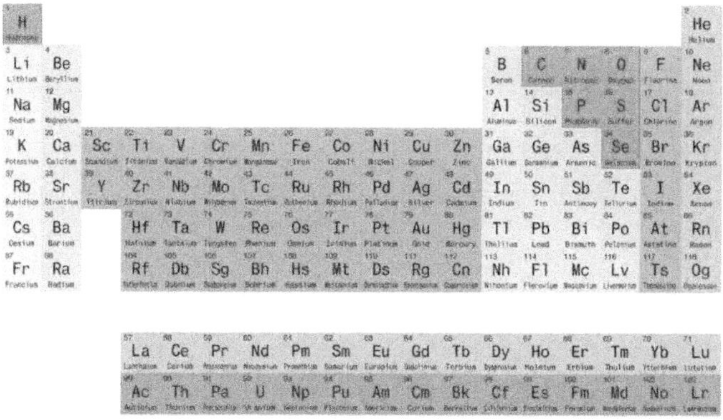

B. Apply the SCALM Technique

1. Structure of the information

In this example, it is not necessary to structure the information as a mind map, because it is already structured by chemists, starting from the creator of this wonderful table of chemical elements, the famous Dmitri Mendeleev.

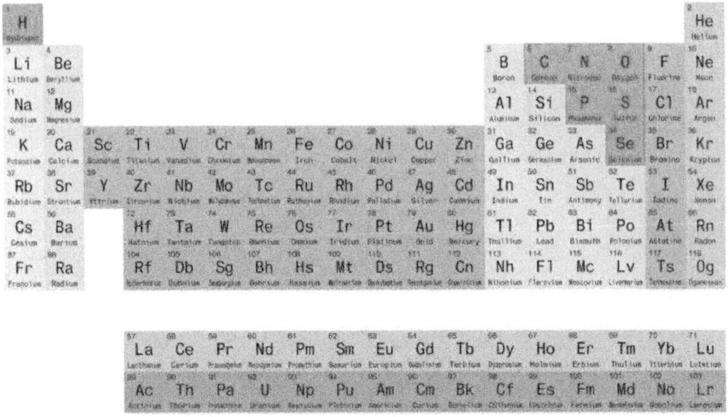

2. Chunk the material

To memorize the periodic table, I will chunk it into 14 chunks (groups of elements) , as follows:

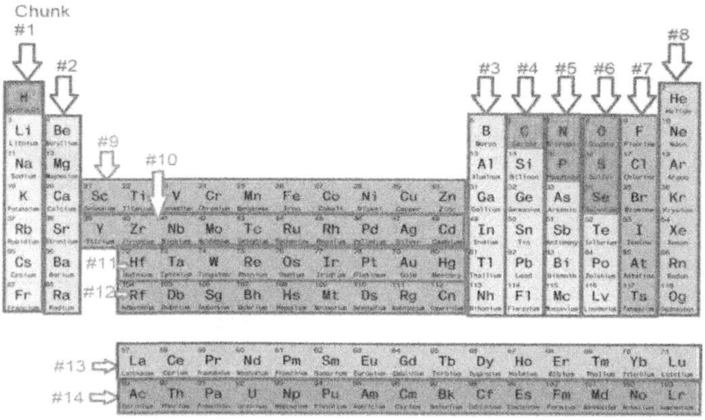

3. Associate the chunks with simple images

By applying *"The Sentence Method"*, each chunk will become a mnemonic phrase, which can easily be imagined by our brains.

Chunks	Associations	Images
Group 1 (H, Li, Na, K, Rb, Cs, Fr)	Hairy Lonely Naked King Robs Constitutional Freedom	

Group 2 (Be, Mg, Ca, Sr, Ba, Ra)	Best Magic Cats Search Bad Rats	
Group 3 (B, Al, Ga, In, Tl, Nh)	Buzz Aldrin Gather Indian Tools (for) Noah	
Group 4 (C, Si, Ge, Sn, Pb, FL)	Charlie Sheen Gets (a) Snowy Pebble Flower	
Group 5 (N, P, As, Sb, Bi, Mc)	New Pope Assign Subordinate Bishops (at) McDonald's.	

Group 6 (O, S, Se, Te, Po, Lv)	Omar Sharif Seems Poor Terribly (in his) Living	
Group 7 (F, Cl, Br, I, At, Ts)	Fidel Castro Breathes Invisible Atoms (from a) Teaspoon	
Group 8 (He, Ne, Ar, Kr, Xe, Rn, Og)	Hercules Nervous Arrives (to) Kill Xenophobic Rangers Organization	
Group 9: (Sc, Ti, V, Cr, Mn, Fe, Co, Ni, Cu, Zn)	Scary Tiny Vicious Creatures Manage Fears to Come Nightly (from) Culpability Zone.	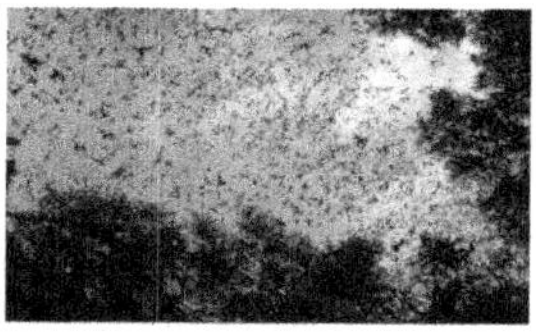

Group 10 : (Y, Zr, Nb, Mo, Tc, Ru, Rh, Pd, Ag, Cd)	Young Zealous Noble Monk Trick Russian RhinostoPredict Aggressive Conditions	
Group 11: (Hf, Ta, W, Re, Os, Ir, Pt, Au, Hg)	Harry Truman Wants to Relax Once Irish Politicians Auction High	
Group 12 : (Rf, Db, Sg, Bh, Hs, Mt, Ds, Rg, Cn)	Rough Doubtful Soldier Bathing in HisModern Designed Rigid Container	
Group 13: (La, Ce, Pr, Nd, Pm, Sm, Eu, Gd, Tb, Dy, Ho, Er, Tm, Yb, Lu)	Lord Cecil Proudly NamedPam, Sam(and) Eugene "the GoodTraditionalistsDying Honorable (for the) Emperor". (The) Team Yell (from their) Lungs	

Group 14: (Ac, Th, Pa, U, Np, Pu, Am, Cm, Bk, Cf, Es, Fm, Md, No, Lr)	Acceleration Throw Planets: Uranus, Neptune, (and) Pluto (in an) Ambush. Coming from Black Cave (is an) Escadrille Formed (in) Middle North Lyra (constellation)	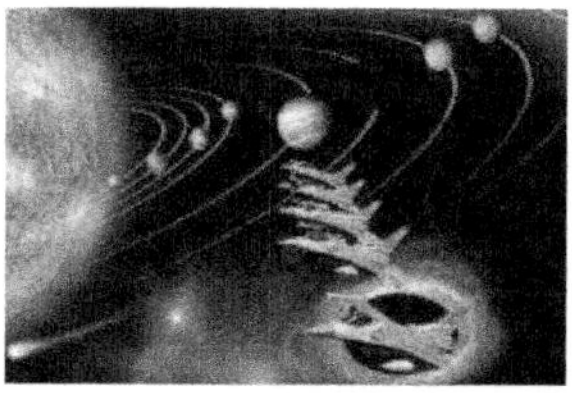

4. Locate (Put the images in a memory palace)

To create your memory palace, choose a journey with 14 stops, arranged in a logical order, in a location that you know very well, like your home.

PS : Probably your home is not that big, but you can choose another well known location for your memory palace, as a public building or a journey through your neighborhood.

5. Memorize the images... and you will know the Periodic Table

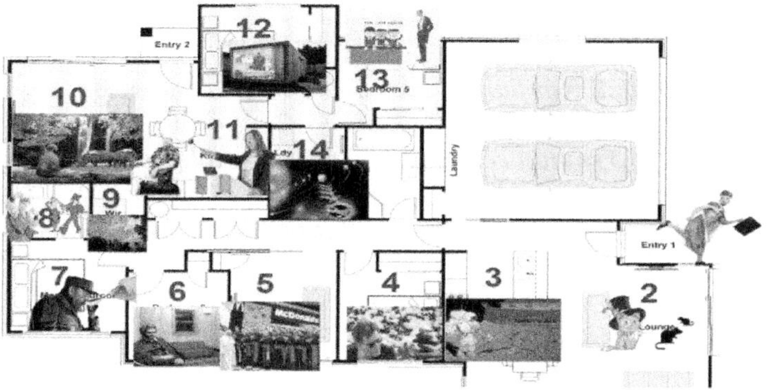

I imagine a running ***naked king*** *at the front door (1) ...,*

then ***a cat (wearing a hat) chasing mouses*** *in the first lounge of the house (2) ...*

Buzz Aldrin gathering Indian tools for Noah *in the kitchen (3)*

Charlie Sheen with a Snowy Pebble Flower *in Bedroom 3 (4)...*

the ***Pope Assign and some Bishops*** *eating McDonald's food in the family room (5) ...*

a poor ***Omar Shariff*** *transforming bedroom 2 in his living room(6)...*

Fidel Castro breathing invisible atoms (from a) teaspoon *in the master bed room (7)....*

A ***Nervous Hercules Killing Xenophobic Rangers*** *in the closet (8)...*

then, I imagine some ***Scary Tiny Vicious Creatures*** *in the walk-in robe(9)...*

a ***Monk with 2 Russian Rhinos*** *in the second lounge(10)* **...**

next, ***Harry Truman*** *relaxing at the kitchen table (11)...*

then a ***Rough Doubtful Soldier Bathing*** *in bedroom number 4(12) ...*

Lord Cecil with the 3 kids *in bedroom number 5(13) ...*

and finally, I imagine ***an escadrille*** *in the last bathroom (14)***.**

Chapter Thirteen: Practical Example #3. Memorize the Atomic Numbers of Chemical Elements

This chapter does not contain an entire step by step application of the SCALM method but is just a supplement to the previous chemistry lesson.

In this chapter, you will learn how to combine two memory techniques you already know, "*The Sound-Alike method*" and "*The Major system*", to memorize the atomic numbers of chemical elements.

We will transform together, into memorable images, the atomic numbers of the first 30 elements, after which you will be able to continue alone, by completing the list of chemical elements.

Let's start with the first chemical element, having the atomic number 1, which is *Hydrogen.*

The name of the element will be transformed, by using The Sound-Alike Method, into a simple image of an object, a person, or an animal.

In this case, I will use the image of "*a hydrant*", which to me sounds very much like "hydrogen".

To memorize the atomic numbers of all chemical elements, I will use a list of numbers from 1 to 118 (because the periodic table contains 118 elements), each number being transformed with the Major System into an easy-to-remember word.

Each digit becomes a consonant, then we create words from the 2 or 3 consonants associated with the numbers. Please note that for numbers from 1 to 9, I will use the variant 01, 02,03, and so on, because we need 2 consonants to create a good word.

So, in the case of *Hydrogen*, we have the number 01, which in the major system becomes the consonants ST or SD. By adding vowels, I can create a word like: *suit, set, or sit*. For me, a memorable image of the hydrogen and its atomic number will be "*a Hydrant dressed in a Suit*"

The second element, having atomic number 2, is *Helium.* For it, I can create the image of *"a helium balloon"*, while the number 02 is S and N in the Major System. SN can become *"a sauna"*, so, for the element Helium, I can create the image of "*a Balloon forgotten in a Sauna*".

The third element is Lithium. For this element, I don't need to use *the Sound Alike Method*, because I can use directly the image of *"a lithium battery"*. The number 03 is SM, which can become *"swim"* or *"sumo"*. I will associate Lithium with the image of "*a Battery fighting Sumo*".

Then, we have Beryllium with the number 04 (SR), which becomes: *"Barry White being knighted "Sir" by the Queen of England"*

As you can see, each image contains two simple and easy to memorize images like objects or persons. It is not advisable to use abstract notions or concepts for our associations, because they can create confusion in your mind. Your brain works with images, these are its alphabet, and simple and concrete images are the easiest to remember

In the next list you will find the rest of the elements up to the atomic number 30, after which you can complete it alone with the images that you think are suitable for your memory.

Remember! The more bizarre and wacky your associations are, the more memorable they will be!

Atomic number	Element name	Sound-alike / memorable image	Major system for numbers		
1	Hydrogen	Hydrant	01	SD,ST	sad/ side/sit/suit/ set
2	Helium	Helium balloon	02	SN	Sean/sun/ sauna/snow/asian
3	Lithium	Battery	03	SM	sum/somo/some/swim
4	Beryllium	Barry White	04	SR	sir/sorrow/Sara
5	Boron	(new) born	05	SL	sail
6	Carbon	Garbo(Greta)	06	SG/SJ/SH	sushi
7	Nitrogen	Night Ray Gun	07	SK	ski
8	Oxygen	diver tube	08	SF/SV	sofa
9	Fluorine	flower	09	SP/SB	USB
10	Neon	light bulb	10	DS/TS	toes
11	Sodium	salt-cellar	11	DD/DT/TD/TT	Teddy

12	Magnesium	magnolia	**12**	DN/TN	Danny
13	Aluminum	airplane	**13**	DM/TM	Tom
14	Silicon	silicone sealant tube	**14**	DR/TR	Audrey
15	Phosphorus	a matchbox	**15**	DL/TL	doll
16	Sulfur	rotten egg	**16**	DJ/DSh/Tch	DJ/dish/touch
17	Chlorine	swimming pool	**17**	DK/TK	duck/tick
18	Argon	air gun	**18**	DF/DV/TF/TV	dove/tofee/tofu/TV
19	Potassium	potty seat	**19**	DP/DB/TP/TB	dope/Dubai/tape/tu ba
20	Calcium	Milk Box	**20**	NS/NZ	news/nose
21	Scandium	stadium	**21**	ND/NT	hand/ant/hunt
22	Titanium	Titanic ship	**22**	NN	nun/nanny/neon
23	Vanadium	JC Van Damme	**23**	NM	name/Nemo
24	Chromium	crown	**24**	NR	Norway/narrow/Ner o
25	Manganese	man with gun	**25**	NL	Neil/nail/noel
26	Iron	Iron Man	**26**	NJ/Nch	inch/ niche/nacho
27	Cobalt	Cobain(Curt)	**27**	NK	ink/neck
28	Nickel	Nick Nolte	**28**	NF/NV	navy/knife
29	Copper	Bradley Cooper	**29**	NP/NB	nap/Newby
30	Zinc	Sink	**30**	MS	mouse/mess
31	Gallium		**31**	MD/MT	mad/meat
32	Germanium		**32**	MN	man/moon/money
33	Arsenic		**33**	MM	mom/Miami
34	Selenium		**34**	MR	Mary/marry
35	Bromine		**35**	ML	mail/mall
36	Krypton		**36**	MG/MCh	image/match
37	Rubidium		**37**	MK	Mickey/Mac
38	Strontium		**38**	MF/MV	Mafia/movie
39	Yttrium		**39**	MP/MB	map/MBA
40	Zirconium		**40**	RS/RZ	race/rice/rose

41	Niobium		**41**	RT/RD	rat/road
42	Molybdenum		**42**	RN	rain/run/iron
43	Technetium		**43**	RM	arm/Rome
44	Ruthenium		**44**	RR	error/warrior
45	Rhodium		**45**	RL	rail/role
46	Palladium		**46**	RG/Rch	rage/rich
47	Silver		**47**	RK	rock
48	Cadmium		**48**	RF/RV	roof/rave
49	Indium		**49**	RB/RP	robe/rap
50	Tin		**50**	LS	loss/Alice
51	Antimony		**51**	LT/LD	light/led/lady
52	Tellurium		**52**	LN	lion/line/alien
53	Iodine		**53**	LM	lime, lama
54	Xenon		**54**	LR	Larry/lawyer/Lyra
55	Cesium		**55**	LL	Lilly/loyal
56	Barium		**56**	LG/Lch/Lsh	algae/leech/leash
57	Lanthanum		**57**	LK	Luke, luck
58	Cerium		**58**	LF/LV	elf/leaf/live/olive
59	Praseodymium		**59**	LP	help/lip
60	Neodymium		**60**	JS/JZ/ChS	jaws/jazz/cheese
61	Promethium		**61**	JT/JD/ChT	jet/judo/chat
62	Samarium		**62**	JN/ChN	join/chain/chin
63	Europium		**63**	JM/ChM	jam/gym/chime
64	Gadolinium		**64**	JR/ChR	jar/chair
65	Terbium		**65**	JL/ChL	jelly/jewel/jail/chill
66	Dysprosium		**66**	JSh/ShSh	Josh/hashish
67	Holmium		**67**	JK/ChK	joke/check
68	Erbium		**68**	JF/ChF	chef
69	Thulium		**69**	JB/JP/ChP	job/jeep/cheap/chip
70	Ytterbium		**70**	KS/KZ	kiss/keys
71	Lutetium		**71**	KT/KD	kite/cat
72	Hafnium		**72**	KN	coin/canoe
73	Tantalum		**73**	KM	kame/Kim

74	Tungsten		**74**	KR	car/curry
75	Rhenium		**75**	KL	coal/cola
76	Osmium		**76**	KG/KCh	cage/coach/cash
77	Iridium		**77**	KK	cacao/coke/cook
78	Platinum		**78**	KF/KV	coffee/cave
79	Gold		**79**	KP/KB	cap/cube/cop
80	Mercury		**80**	FC/FS/VS/VZ	face/vase
81	Thallium		**81**	FT/FD/VT/VD	fat/feet/food
82	Lead		**82**	FN/VN	fun/fan
83	Bismuth		**83**	FM/VM	fame/foam
84	Polonium		**84**	FR/VR	fire/fry
85	Astatine		**85**	FL/VL	fall/fuel/villa
86	Radon		**86**	FJ/FCh/VJ	Fiji/fish/voyage
87	Francium		**87**	FG/VG	fog/vogue
88	Radium		**88**	FF/FV/VF/VV	fief/five/viva
89	Actinium		**89**	FB/FP/VB/VP	FBI/phobia/VIP
90	Thorium		**90**	BS/BZ/PS/PZ	boss/bus/buzz/peas
91	Protactinium		**91**	BT/BD/PT/PD	bat/bed/pet/pad
92	Uranium		**92**	BN/PN	bean/bunny/pen
93	Neptunium		**93**	BM/PM	beam/puma
94	Plutonium		**94**	BR/PR	beer/bear/pear/pray
95	Americium		**95**	BL/PL	ball/pool
96	Curium		**96**	BSh/Pch	bush/peach
97	Berkelium		**97**	BK/PK	bike/book
98	Californium		**98**	BF/BV/PF/PV	beef/puff
99	Einsteinium		**99**	BB/PP/BP/PB	baby/pipe
100	Fermium		**100**	DSS/TSS	disease/disuse/theses/thesis
101	Mendelevium		**101**	DST/TST	dust/tasty/test/twist
102	Nobelium		**102**	DSN/TSN	Disney/ Edison/Watson
103	Lawrencium		**103**	DSM/TSM	atheism/ autism/Taoism
104	Rutherfordium		**104**	DSR/TSR	desire/ teaser/ tzar
105	Dubnium		**105**	DSL/TSL	diesel/Tesla

106	Seaborgium		**106**	DSG/TSG	disguise
107	Bohrium		**107**	DSK/TSK	disco/task/Tusk
108	Hassium		**108**	DSV/TSF	adhesive/ theosophy
109	Meitnerium		**109**	DSB/TSB	disobey
110	Darmstadtium		**110**	DDS/TDS	tweeds/duds
111	Roentgenium		**111**	TTD/DDT	attitude/tattooed
112	Copernicium		**112**	DTN/TTN	addition/Titan
113	Ununtrium		**113**	DTM/TTM	daytime/totem
114	Flerovium		**114**	DTR/TTR	Tatra/ auditor/theatre
115	Ununpentium		**115**	DTL/TTM	deadly/detail/total
116	Livermorium		**116**	DTCh/TTCh	ditch/Dutch /twitch
117	Ununseptium		**117**	DDG/TDG	dodge/hotdog
118	Ununoctium		**118**	DDF/DTV	detoxify/oxidative

But, how do you store these images so that they remain in your long-term memory?The answer is simple: You put them in a memory palace!

Choose a journey through a well-known area, and, in the places that stand out (bus stations, shops, petrol stations, etc.), you put your memorable images and link them with the location. This way, you will be able to memorize all the elements in order. If you think the number of locations in your memory palace is too great, you may have trouble remembering all of them. If so, try combining two or three images at one location. By placing

3 images in each location, you will need a 40 stops journey to store all 118 chemical elements, which is quite easy to do.

Chapter Fourteen: Practical Example #4. Memorize a Biology Lesson

A. The Learning Material (A Biology Lesson)

Characteristics of living things

" ***Complex organization***

Living things have a level of complexity and organization not found in lifeless objects. At its most fundamental level, a living thing is composed of one or more cells. These units, generally too small to be seen with the naked eye, are organized into tissues. A tissue is a series of cells that accomplish a shared function. Tissues, in turn, form organs, such as the stomach and kidney. A number of organs working together compose an organ system. An organism is a complex series of various organ systems.

Metabolism

Living things exhibit a rapid turnover of chemical materials, which is referred to as **metabolism.** *Metabolism involves exchanges of chemical matter with the external environment and extensive transformations of organic matter within the cells of a living organism. Metabolism generally involves the release or use of* *chemical energy. Nonliving things do not display metabolism.*

Responsiveness

All living things are able to respond to stimuli in the external environment. For example, living things respond to changes in light, heat, sound, and chemical and mechanical contact. To detect stimuli, organisms have means for receiving information, such as eyes, ears, and taste buds. To respond effectively to changes in the environment, an organism must coordinate its responses. A system of nerves and a number of chemical regulators called **hormones** *coordinate activities within an organism. The organism responds to the stimuli by means of a number of effectors, such as muscles and glands. Energy is generally used in the process. Organisms change their behavior in response to changes in the surrounding environment. For example, an organism may move in response to its environment. Responses such as this occur in definite patterns and make up the behavior of an organism. The behavior is active, not passive; an animal responding to a stimulus is different from a stone rolling down a hill. Living things display* ***responsiveness;*** *nonliving things do not.*

Growth

Growth requires an organism to take in material from the environment and organize the material into its own structures. To accomplish growth, an organism expends some of the energy it acquires during metabolism. An organism has a pattern for accomplishing the building of growth structures.During growth, a living organism transforms material that is unlike itself into materials that are like it. A person, for example, digests a meal of meat and vegetables and transforms the chemical material into more of himself or herself. A nonliving organism does not display this characteristic.

Reproduction

A living thing has the ability to produce copies of itself by the process known as reproduction. These copies are made while the organism is still living. Among plants and simple animals, reproduction is often an extension of the growth process. More complex organisms engage in a type of reproduction called sexual reproduction, in which two parents contribute to the formation of a new individual. During this process, a new combination of traits can be produced. Asexual reproduction involves only one parent, and the resulting cells are generally identical to the parent cell. For example, bacteria grow and quickly reach maturity, after which they split into two organisms by a process of asexual reproduction called binary fission.

Evolution

Living organisms have the ability to adapt to their environment through the process of evolution. During evolution, changes occur in populations, and the organisms in the population become better able to metabolize, respond, and reproduce. They develop abilities to cope with their environment that their ancestors did not have. Evolution also results in a greater variety of organisms than existed in previous eras. This proliferation of populations of organisms is unique to living things.

Ecology

The environment influences the living things that it surrounds. Ecology is the study of relationships between organisms and their relationships with their environment. Both biotic factors (living things) and abiotic factors (nonliving things) can alter the environment. Rain and sunlight are non-living components, for example, that greatly influence the environment. Living things may migrate or hibernate if the environment becomes difficult to live in."

B. Apply the SCALM Technique

1. Structure of the information

Let's create an overview of the material as a Mind Map:

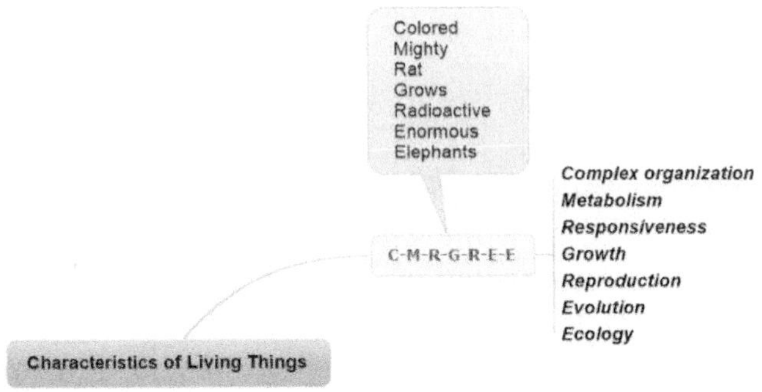

To remember the 7 key factors, use the Sentence Method, and get this phrase:

"Colored Mighty Rat Grows Radioactive Enormous Elephants"

2. Chunk the material

The Chunks:
Complex organization Living things have a level of complexity and organization not found in lifeless objects. At its most fundamental level, a living thing is composed of one or more **cells.** These units, generally too small to be seen with the naked eye, are organized into tissues. A *tissue* is a series of cells that accomplish a shared function. Tissues, in turn, form *organs,* such as the stomach and kidney. A number of organs working together compose an *organ system.* An *organism* is a complex series of various organ systems.
Metabolism Living things exhibit a rapid turnover of chemical materials, which is referred to as **metabolism.** Metabolism involves exchanges of chemical matter with the external environment and extensive transformations of organic matter within the cells of a living organism. Metabolism generally involves the release or use of chemical energy. Nonliving things do not display metabolism.
Responsiveness All living things are able to respond to stimuli in the external environment. For example, living things respond to changes in light, heat, sound, and chemical and mechanical contact. To detect

stimuli, organisms have means for receiving information, such as eyes, ears, and taste buds.

To respond effectively to changes in the environment, an organism must coordinate its responses. A system of nerves and a number of chemical regulators called **hormones** coordinate activities within an organism. The organism responds to the stimuli by means of a number of effectors, such as muscles and glands. Energy is generally used in the process.

Organisms change their behavior in response to changes in the surrounding environment. For example, an organism may move in response to its environment. Responses such as this occur in definite patterns and make up the behavior of an organism. The behavior is active, not passive; an animal responding to a stimulus is different from a stone rolling down a hill. Living things display **responsiveness;** nonliving things do not.

Growth

Growth requires an organism to take in material from the environment and organize the material into its own structures. To accomplish growth, an organism expends some of the energy it acquires during metabolism.

An organism has a pattern for accomplishing the building of growth structures.

During growth, a living organism transforms material that is unlike itself into materials that are like it. A person, for example, digests a meal of meat and vegetables and transforms the chemical material into more of himself or herself. A nonliving organism does not display this characteristic.

Reproduction

A living thing has the ability to produce copies of itself by the process known as *reproduction.* These copies are made while the organism is still living. Among plants and simple animals, reproduction is often an extension of the growth process.

More complex organisms engage in a type of reproduction called *sexual reproduction,* in which two parents contribute to the formation of a new individual. During this process, a new combination of traits can be produced.

Asexual reproduction involves only one parent, and the resulting cells are generally identical to the parent cell. For example, bacteria grow and quickly reach maturity, after which they split into two organisms by a process of asexual reproduction called *binary fission.*

Evolution

Living organisms have the ability to adapt to their environment through the process of evolution. During evolution, changes occur in populations, and the organisms in the population become better able to metabolize, respond, and reproduce. They develop abilities to cope with their environment that their ancestors did not have.

Evolution also results in a greater variety of organisms than existed in previous eras. This proliferation of populations of organisms is unique to living things.

Ecology
The environment influences the living things that it surrounds. *Ecology* is the study of relationships between organisms and their relationships with their environment. Both biotic factors (living things) and abiotic factors (nonliving things) can alter the environment. Rain and sunlight are non-living components, for example, that greatly influence the environment. Living things may migrate or hibernate if the environment becomes difficult to live in.

3. Associate the chunks with simple images

The Chunks	The Associations	The Images
Complex organization Living things have a level of complexity and organization not found in lifeless objects. At its most fundamental level, a living thing is composed of one or more ***cells.*** These units, generally too small to be seen with the naked eye, are organized into tissues. A ***tissue*** is a series of cells that accomplish a shared function. Tissues, in turn, form ***organs,*** such as the	**Use The Sentence method for this list :** • Cells • Tissues • Organs • Organ Systems • Organism and get this phrase:	

stomach and kidney. A number of organs working together compose an ***organ system***. An ***organism*** is a complex series of various organ systems.	***"Complicated Tests Obtain ObeSe Oranges"***	
Metabolism		
Living things exhibit a rapid turnover of chemical materials, which is referred to as **metabolism.** Metabolism involves **exchanges** of **chemical matter** with the external environment and extensive **transformations of organic matter within the cells** of a living organism.	Exchange = dolar bill Chemical matter =a *chemical discharge pipe* transformations = butterfly in prison(cell)	  
Metabolism generally involves the release or use of chemical energy.	chemical energy= battery	
Nonliving things do not display metabolism.	black computer screen	

Responsiveness All living things are able to respond to stimuli in the external environment.	telephone ringing	
For example, living things respond to changes in light, heat, sound, chemical and mechanical contact.	**The Sentence method:** "Large Hummingbird Smells Colorful Matches"	
To detect stimuli, organisms have means for receiving information, such as eyes, ears, and taste buds.	a metal detector with eyes , ears and mouth	
To respond effectively to changes in the environment, an organism must coordinate its responses. A system of nerves and a number of chemical regulators called **hormones** coordinate	nervous - bodybuilder – checking coordinates on a GPS	

activities within an organism.		
The organism responds to the stimuli by means of a number of effectors, such as muscles and glands. Energy is generally used in the process.	Effector – sound alike "F- actor" – Image Frank Sinatra showing his muscles to Glenn Miller to get an Energy drink	 
Organisms change their behavior in response to changes in the surrounding environment. For example, an organism may move in response to its environment. Responses such as this occur in definite patterns and make up the behavior of an organism. The behavior is active, not passive; an animal responding to a stimulus is different from a stone rolling down a hill. Living things display **responsiveness;** nonliving things do not.	A man with an umbrella running in the *rain* *A dog running from a* stone rolling down a hill	 

Growth		
Growth requires an organism to take in material from the environment and organize the material into its own structures. To accomplish growth, an organism expends some of the energy it acquires during metabolism.	A flower growing in a red bull can	
An organism has a pattern for accomplishing the building of growth structures.	A snail	
During growth, a living organism transforms material that is unlike itself into materials that are like it. A person, for example, digests a meal of meat and vegetables and transforms the chemical material into more of himself or herself. A nonliving organism does not display this characteristic.	A meal of meat and vegetables into a chemistry glassware	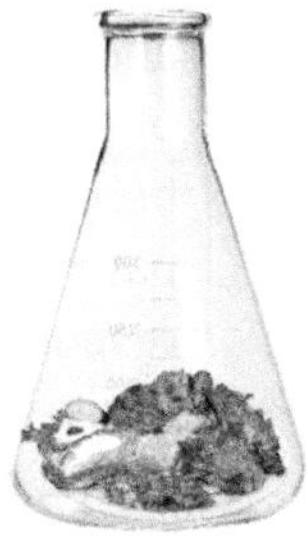

Reproduction A living thing has the ability to produce copies of itself by the process known as *reproduction.* These copies are made while the organism is still living. Among plants and simple animals, reproduction is often an extension of the growth process.	A Xerox machine	
More complex organisms engage in a type of reproduction called *sexual reproduction,* in which two parents contribute to the formation of a new individual. During this process, a new combination of traits can be produced.	You're free to choose your image :))	
Asexual reproduction involves only one parent, and the resulting cells are generally identical to the parent cell. For example, bacteria grow and quickly reach maturity, after	A Eunuch	

which they split into two organisms by a process of asexual reproduction called *binary fission.*		
Evolution Living organisms have the ability to adapt to their environment through the process of evolution. During evolution, changes occur in populations, and the organisms in the population become better able to metabolize, respond, and reproduce. They develop abilities to cope with their environment that their ancestors did not have. Evolution also results in a greater variety of organisms than existed in previous eras. This proliferation of populations of organisms is unique to living things.	A Chameleon An M&M's bag	 

Ecology The environment influences the living things that it surrounds. *Ecology* is the study of relationships between organisms and their relationships with their environment. Both biotic factors (living things) and abiotic factors (nonliving things) can alter the environment. Rain and sunlight are non-living components, for example, that greatly influence the environment.	A Tree half under the sun and half under the rain	
Living things may migrate or hibernate if the environment becomes difficult to live in.	A Bear hibernating	

4. Locate (Put the images in a memory palace)

To memorize the images in order, I will use a memory palace to place my images. The most common type of memory palace involves making a mental journey through a familiar place like your home or your town. Along that journey, there are specific locations that you always visit in the same order, so you can create a path in your mind's eye, made up of places that you know well, and can easily visualize, then populate this places with images representing whatever you want to remember.

I can use my daily route to school as a memory palace:

In the front door of my house, I **imagine a scientist doing experiments with an obese orange (1)** ....then **a dollar bill (2), a chemical discharge pipe**(3), and **an imprisoned butterfly(4)** in the next house on my route.

A battery (**5**) and a big **blank computer screen (6)** near the next house... **a telephone ringing(7)** in front of the greenhouse ... a "*Large Hummingbird Smelling some Colorful Matches*" **(8)** on the roof of next building...then a **smiling metal detector (9)** on this wall...and here we come to the bridge, where I imagine a **nervous bodybuilder(10)** ... and **Frank Sinatra along with Glenn Miller(11)** under the bridge.

Then, I imagine **a man with an umbrella running in the rain(12)** ...and **a dog running from a stone rolling down a hill(13)**, behind the next house.

In front of the police station, there is a big **Red bull can with a flower (14)** .... And further on, in front of the fire station, I can Imagine **a big Snail(15)** attacking the firemen.

On the roof of the hospital building, I can imagine a **big chemistry glassware containing a meal of meat and vegetables** (**16**)... then, **a Xerox machine(17)** falls from the roof of this tall building. On the second floor of this building, there are some **sexual activities(18)**...., while in front of the city hall I can imagine **a eunuch(19)** waiting for the mayor to hire him.

On the roof of the next building, I can imagine an oversized **chameleon (20)**...and in front of this tower, I can see **a large bag of M & M's (21).**

At the top of the tower, there is **a tree located half under the sun and half under the rain(22)** ... and finally, on the school stairs, **a bear hibernates(23).**

So, we have 23 memorable images, which we placed along a mental journey that will help us to memorize them in order, and we almost memorized them. This tangled biology lesson has been transformed into easy-to-remember images.

5. Memorize the images... and you will know your Lesson

At this stage, you walk on our mental journey again, visualizing the mental images. These weird pictures will stick like glue in your memory and all the associated concepts will appear immediately in your mind's eye.

Chapter Fifteen: Tips and Tricks for Practicing the SCALM Technique

In this chapter, I will teach you some tips and tricks to help you become more efficient in using the SCALM method.

1. **Learn and do!**

Start by learning the technique, and then practice it thoroughly. Only then can you use it to its full potential. With this method, your learning process can be fun, and you can achieve astonishingly impressive results very quickly. Each of the memory techniques you have learned in this course can be practiced separately and can help you in many situations.

Here are some examples:

Mind maps can be used to classify, visualize, and at times generate ideas to solve problems and make better decisions. A mind map is a creative and effective tool to put information into your brain and to take information out of your brain, which maps out' your thoughts and your projects

The Sound-Alike Method is great for memorizing the vocabulary of any foreign language you want to learn.

Acronyms and The Sentence Method are very effective for memorizing shopping lists orto-do lists.

Everyday Numbers such as Credit Card Numbers, PINs, Bank account numbers, Combinations for locks and safes, Telephone numbers, Computer passwords, can be easily memorized using *The Major System.*

The Major System can also help you create and keep your own mental calendar for appointments and anniversaries. With this mental calendar, you will have the dates for your work schedule, the birthdays of your friends, and other important dates imprinted in your mind, and you won't have to write them down.

The ability to remember people's names with *The Names Association Technique* is an incredibly useful skill, in business and social interactions that will increase your self-confidence.

Please remember that learning is a proactive process. We learn by doing and by practicing the learning tools. If you want to master the SCALM technique, do something about it. Apply it at every opportunity. If you don't, you will forget it!

2. Be flexible!

You can adapt the method to suit your style. Your ability to adapt to the memory techniques will increase with practice. You may also want to consider integrating some other memory techniques, more suited to your learning style. You can use whatever you want, as long as it helps your learning and recall.

3. Prepare your toolkit

If you want to use the SCALM method for large and different materials, you may consider creating (in advance) your collection of memory palaces, each meant to memorize a certain type of information.

If the number of locations becomes too great, you may also consider putting two or three images together in a single location of the memory palace.

As memory experts do, you can use the same memory palace more than once if there is a time-lapse between the different items you want to remember, particularly if you are going to use a set of completely different items. Sometimes, when reusing a memory palace, your brain can become confused as to which of the images was right for that sequence. This is a well-known phenomenon called "*Ghosts on Location*". But, with a sufficient time delay between two uses of the same memory palace, your memory from one list, generally, won't interfere with your memory of the next set of items, but in the meantime, it is recommended to develop your own collection of different memory palaces and rotate their use.

4. Side effects

If you consistently apply the SCALM technique, in addition to improving your learning skills and your memory, you will notice an improvement in the overall quality of your life. Because this method trains your brain's capacity to manipulate mental images, it will become easier for you to think creatively, to generate images, ideas, and thoughts and to make faster and better decisions in all areas of your life.

Finally, remember the Essence of the SCALM Technique:

All you have to do is follow the 5 steps to create memorable associations, and then place them along a mental journey. The method is simple, but not always easy. As I told you from the beginning of the book, this method does not offer a miraculous solution to memorize information, as many photo-reading techniques claim to do.

The SCALM learning process is proactive, involving a mental work of deconstructing, organizing, and reconstructing the material, but all these are part of the natural process of efficient learning.

What I can tell you for sure is that the SCALM method is the most efficient way to learn large volumes of information accurately and for long periods.

See you in the next chapter for the summary!

Summary

We've covered a lot of topics in this book.

The SCALM method was presented in a step by step, sequential, manner.

I hope my attempt to come up with as much detail as possible did not confuse you.

In essence, the SCALM method is very simple and is very versatile, its five steps following the natural learning path of the brain:

1. Structure of the information
2. Chunk it into small manageable pieces
3. Associate each chunk with a concrete and easy to remember the image
4. Place the images along a mental journey and
5. Memorize them in order.

Even if the examples presented here were quite short, suitable for an introductory course on this method, the same sequence of steps can be applied for learning whole books. The only difference will be that, after you structure the material into a general mind map, you will need to divide the book into chapters, and then apply the SCALM method to each chapter as if it were a separate material. You will have a smaller mind map, as well as a separate memory palace, for each chapter. In this way, the learning material will be compartmentalized and structured for efficient learning.

I believe that SCALM is more than another learning method. It is a generator of new possibilities and opportunities that can open up new directions in your studies or your career.

Because it combines many advanced memory techniques, practicing it should help you internalize many memory improvement principles and it will pave the way for you to become a super learner and even a memory athlete.

At this point, you might be wondering… what next? If this book is over, what are the next steps on this journey towards a better memory? And when does it end?

Since none of us are perfect or will ever be, there is always a way for us to improve. If memory improvement will become your hobby, you'll continue to improve it over time, and this is a process that continues all your life. The journey of memory improvement does not end. But it does get more interesting because you will start to think more clearly and faster, you will be able to make better decisions and your self-confidence will increase.

I recommend you visit my blog, *"The Mnemo Bay",* where you can find the most complete and orderly collection of materials on this field of memory improvement: books, video courses, memory techniques, memory foods and drinks, memory supplements, and many more. To stay up to date with my future projects, just subscribe to my blog, and I will keep you informed about them.

You might also be interested in my online courses (you can find them on my blog), dedicated to the most important memory techniques. These courses can make you understand better what memory improvement is about, and see for yourself just how simple and handy this skill is. You will find simple techniques that you can apply in your daily life, but also advanced methods used by memory experts in competitions, that can help you achieve amazing results with your memory.

So, if you were waiting for the perfect time to begin your memory improvement journey, the time is now. This course gave you all the tools to do it and you can start today!

Final Words

"I would like to thank you for your interest and your time.

I wish you well, in memory improvement and life.

Keep improving your memory and keep learning"

Chris M Nemo
Creator of the SCALM Technique
Memory Improvement Writer and Blogger

About the Author

My name is **Chris M Nemo** and I'm a Memory Improvement Writer & Blogger.

I'm passionate about helping you to achieve more with your mind right now, regardless of your education, age, or other conditionings.

After studying dozens of books, totaling some thousands of pages, dozens of hours of e-learning courses, and hundreds of hours of practical exercises in this field of memory improvement, I decided to share this knowledge with people interested in learning this skill.

I'm also the creator of the **Super Clever Advanced Learning Method (SCALM)**, a universal method that can help you learn any subject and even memorize entire books. Combining the most efficient memory techniques, this original method is extremely efficient and versatile.

On my blog, *"The Mnemo Bay"*, you can find an organized framework for everything related to memory improvement, which can give you a clear picture of what this wonderful hobby and skill can do for your life.

If you decide to learn and practice the SCALM technique or other memory improvement techniques, I can *guide you* through this process with my experience. You'll find *me* at *my blog, The Mnemo Bay-* www.mnemobay.com *, on Facebook or Twitter.*

You can e-mail me anytime at mnemobay@gmail.com .

My Online Courses

Based on the old saying *"a picture is worth a thousand words"* , Dr. James McQuivey has made this number juggling:

"A picture equals 1,000 words. Video shoots 30 frames per second. Therefore, every second of video is worth 30,000 words. Multiply 30k by 60 seconds – a common length for an explainer video – and you get 1.8 million words, which means 3,600 pages of text!"

I am convinced that the future of education is based on e-learning courses, so I focused my creative efforts on creating valuable online courses.

On my blog, The Mnemo Bay, you will find a lot of easy-to-follow courses that I have created to promote memory techniques and to unravel this rather hermetic field of memory training.

In the first place, you will find a course dedicated to the Super Clever Advanced Learning Method (SCALM), where you can practice this effective method in a more appealing environment.

My biggest course, "The Complete Memory Improvement Course- Your Ultimate Guide to a Stronger Memory", is also available there. With over 7 hours of video lessons and a lot of resources included, this course is a complete guide to memory improvement. From ancient memory techniques to modern World Memory Championships, you can find everything here that may be of interest to you.

The Mnemo Bay also offers many practical courses for beginners and advanced students. To keep up to date on the latest news, visit my blog and subscribe for free to keep up with the latest information.

My goal is to create simple to understand, but at the same time full of solid content courses, to make you understand better what memory improvement is about, and see for yourself just how simple and handy this skill is.

If you want to have a better memory, just choose your favorite course and enroll. You have a 30-day money back guarantee if you don't like it. I'm always improving my courses so that they stay up to date and the best that they can be.

*****______*****______*****_____*****